A

SEMI-CENTENARY DISCOURSE,

DELIVERED IN

THE FIRST AFRICAN PRESBYTERIAN CHURCH, PHILADELPHIA,

ON THE FOURTH SABBATH OF MAY, 1857:

WITH

A HISTORY

OF THE CHURCH FROM ITS FIRST ORGANIZATION:

INCLUDING

A BRIEF NOTICE OF REV. JOHN GLOUCESTER, ITS FIRST PASTOR.

BY REV. WILLIAM T. CATTO,

PASTOR.

ALSO,

AN APPENDIX,

Containing sketches of all the Colored Churches in Philadelphia.

PHILADELPHIA:

JOSEPH M. WILSON,

No. 111 SOUTH TENTH STREET, BELOW CHESTNUT.

1857.

NOTICE.

On motion of Rev. Dr. Boardman, it was

Resolved, "That the Presbytery have learned, with satisfaction, that the Rev. Wm. T. Catto has prepared for publication an account of the First African Presbyterian Church, and cordially recommend his historical sketch to the patronage of all who feel interested in the religious welfare of the colored population of our country."

A true extract from the *Minutes of the Presbytery of Philadelphia*, at their session in West Spruce Street Church, Philadelphia, July 6, 1857.

Attest: DANIEL GASTON,
Stated Clerk.

DISCOURSE.

Speak unto the children of Israel that they go forward.—*Ex.* xiv. 15.

I HAVE chosen this subject for the occasion on account of its scope. What to the children of Abraham under their peculiar situation, may to the people of God, in this day, be as important.

Go forward, as a command from the mouth of God, is worthy of our deepest consideration, and should be regarded as worthy of all acceptation by a nation, a community, a sect, or a church, and should by the individual man, in his life, practice, example, faith, grace, knowledge, wisdom, truth, and holiness.

What I purpose upon this occasion is—

I. To notice the circumstance that gave rise to the text—that briefly.

II. The command as it affects the individual.

III. The command as it touches a church, and the history of this church.

I. It is known to you all that the children of Israel were in captivity in Egypt, and remained in that condition upwards of 220 years. The sequel of their bondage shows that their condition was one of affliction and distress: their repeated cries and supplications to God make this assertion as clear as a sunbeam. To such an extent did their oppressors torment them by exacting the severest labor and most cruel demands, that their cries ascended to God, and he determined to deliver them.

To this end Moses was raised up as a leader and deliverer of this people. Now the circumstance of Moses being raised up is as singular as it is interesting: a brief sketch of it in this discourse may not be out of place, as there seemingly are some points of it analogous to the life of Mr. Gloucester, the founder of this church.

Moses was of a family of the oppressed, and as far as human estimate considers it, was of humble origin: still he was chosen by the Almighty as the future instrument to bring about a deliverance for these bondmen. The miraculous manner of his preservation from the cruel and heartless order of Pharaoh is a peculiarity worthy of notice: his being placed in an ark of bulrushes—a very fragile vessel—and then set upon the margin of the river among the flags, and there found by Pharaoh's daughter. His preservation and education by the princess is also worthy of thought, and will show that God chooses instruments, ways and means to bring about his purposes which to human speculation is the most improbable: yet is it true, simple and improbable as it may appear; but they are sure in their results, and fail not.

So it appears in the case under consideration. Israel was to be delivered from bondage; a leader was wanting; that leader was, and must be a man possessing peculiar traits of character—a peculiar man, necessary and fitted for the work—every feature of character was to stamp him as the man for the occasion and the business.

And how well did God produce in Moses these peculiar traits; how completely did he regulate, direct, and control every event in order to accomplish the end;—brought up in Pharaoh's house, under the parental watchings of his own mother, wittingly introduced as a nurse, his education perfected, through the king's daughter, and that education a liberal and finished one, are surely very remarkable. Then consider his meekness, the softness of manners, the inflexible integrity of his heart, his great firmness, his courage and boldness, his deep love for his people, and his faith in God, are so many proofs by which we conclude the man was fitted for the work. It does not require much insight into human affairs to determine that the above traits of character must exist in a man who would lead in a measure of importance. The rise of empires, kingdoms, and republics are proofs in point. It requires a stout heart, strong arms, and much firmness to grasp the helm of affairs and steer forward amid dangers and liabilities until success shall crown the effort.

Arrived at the age of manhood, God informs Moses that he is chosen as a leader of his people. The subsequent message to King Pharaoh; the wonderful things done by God to bring the king to his senses in order to restore the people their liberty, to undo their heavy burdens, &c., you are informed of, and how faithfully their leader performed his duty. You have knowledge of their final departure from Egypt to a land of freedom, the land of Canaan, where they could worship God under their own vine and fig-tree, none to molest or make them afraid, and we can well imagine what their hopes and anticipations were when they found their journey toward the promised land really begun, as in their tribes and families they take up the line of march.

During their journey Moses, at the command of God, caused the people to turn in before Pi-hahiroth, between Migdol and the sea, &c., and there encamp themselves. It was during this encampment that Pharaoh regretted having liberated the Israelites, and he determined to pursue them and drive them back to Egypt, which he accordingly attempted: his horsemen and chariots and his army were soon gathered, and he went in pursuit of the Israelites. Seeing the Egyptians pursuing, they began to murmur and complain against Moses; they became very uneasy at the sight of their enemies, and regretted having left Egypt.

Now it is true God commanded them to encamp, and it was during that very time that the enemy appeared; hence it may be inferred that their dilemma was not brought about by any act of theirs; so that they being found resting when they should have been journeying was not their fault. To this, in view of the text, we find no objection; the only exception is their mistrust of God, and want of confidence in their leader, by complaining and reproaching Moses for the danger in which they were placed. Moses too, though not mistrustful of God, sought in the first place to allay their fears, and so check their murmurs and reproaches—an evident delay that might have been better employed, for it is plain that it was a time for action, a time that should have been employed in fleeing from the pursuer, and extricating themselves from their trouble. This will appear still more evident by tracing further the course taken by Moses, and the order he received from God. After first trying to quiet the fears of the people, he next addresses himself to God. Whereupon the Lord said unto him, "Wherefore criest thou unto me? speak unto the children of Israel that they go forward." As though it were said, Lose no time, improve every moment, cry as you go forward, the enemy is behind you, your course is before you, though it be through the sea go forward, and lose no time, and look to me for deliverance and success. The sequel of this incident in the history of this people you all know: they did go forward, their difficulties were removed, for the sea was made to part at the lifting up of Moses' rod over it, and the people went through safely; which their pursuers essaying to do, were overwhelmed and destroyed.

II. I call your attention to these words as they affect the individual man. I adopt this course as you can plainly see that a community or an army, a nation or a church, are comprised of individuals, each man making up the aggregate, and therefore upon the life, conduct, and action of each man depend, in a greater or lesser degree, the power and influence of the whole, whether it be a nation, an army, or a church.

Now as it regards individuals, we assume that no man in the great world of life and action can be idle and indifferent to the callings and claims of government; regarding men as citizens, members of society, heads of families, or in the relation of friends, it cannot with any show of truth be said upon him there are no claims. Every man, more or less, has some part to perform in the drama of life; there can be no stand, no rest, no indifference on this active, busy, working stage; the world is ever moving, and everything around shows life, activity, energy, commotion; the world goes forward in numerous almost countless operations; its motto is forward. As individuals we must go forward upon the broad bosom of this ocean life and contribute our something towards the press of interests that impels forward: who moves not will be pushed aside, or irresistibly borne forward, uncared for and unhonored: we all must struggle in this race of active life, and add our quota to the universal use. The command is a good one, Go forward, and wise is the man who obeys it. Observation with its keen eye, attentive ear, comprehensive intellect, and sound judgment, attests the fact that in order to accomplish any purpose or attain any end, the individual man must go forward to insure success and grasp his desire. No aim in life can be successful without it. If in quest of wealth or position, science, literature, or anything else, earnest perseverance as well as strong resolution, activity and energy, are necessary forces, and must be brought out for the struggle. Is the aim intellectual greatness, the command Go forward holds good; attention, assiduity, application, are elements necessary to crown the effort. In the life of each man the command is good; to him it is as essential as any law of his being. Old habits, if they are injurious in their tendency by corrupting the heart in any way, must be broken off, and a sound morality, virtuous and upright deportment, must mark the general character.

Particularly is this command good in the Christian man's life. The commandment of the Lord is pure, enlightening the eyes. Every professing Christian must grow in grace and in knowledge—knowledge of himself, of his God, of his obligations to the world around him, and as to matters of faith grow therein. Paul says—"Brethren, I count not myself to have apprehended, but this one thing I do, forgetting those things which are behind, and reaching forth unto those things which are before, I press toward the mark for the prize of the high calling of God in Christ Jesus."

Viewing the principle plainly taught in this text as it bears upon the individual man, we must admit its importance and necessity, as it enters into every arrangement introduced for his government by Jehovah himself. He writes it in fairest lines drawn upon every effort to benefit the moral or the Christian world—progress, progression, is the seal of God itself, whereby is stamped the likeness and image of that Being who gave to Moses the command Go forward. It does seem that God, through every progress made, whether in the arts or sciences, whether in the church or state, only reiterates what he said to Moses whilst they were resting before Baal Zephon. And from amid this world of life, where all are in commotion, and each one agitated upon its troubled bosom, pushing his way through the laboring multitudes, shall we single out the Christian man and say to him as the representative of a class of that busy world, you are an exception, whilst others should go forward you may stand still: this can never be; the Christian man can no more stand idle amid the conflicts of life than the earth on which he dwells can cease its revolutions and exist. Every one of us has work to do, around us as well as within us. We begin in childhood to act our part upon the stage of life: as we grow in age, in size, in strength, so grows our labor; as we develop our physical and mental man, so must we produce qualifications necessary for the employments and engagements of life, every man for his calling, as Paul records it. "But the manifestation of the spirit is given to every man to profit withal: for to one is given, by the spirit, the word of wisdom; to another the word of knowledge, by the same spirit; to another faith, by the same spirit; to another the gifts of healing, by the same spirit; to another the working of miracles; to another prophecy; to another discerning of spirits; to another divers kinds of tongues; to another the interpretation of tongues: but all these worketh that one and the selfsame spirit, dividing to every man severally as he will." There is therefore an obligation upon every Christian professor, a necessity of going forward in every calling, whether of faith or practice; to make progress—plain, unmistakable progress, such as will be seen, felt, and acknowledged by all. These should be so plain as to mark the Christian in his life and efforts to advance the interest of humanity and the glory of his God. This is, in fact, the chief end of man.

III. The command in its scope touches governments and communities as well as individuals, they too must go forward in the march of life. It is as necessary in all that concerns their interests as the individual. They should go forward from a state of barbarism to enlightened civilization, from heathen superstition to a knowledge of the Christian graces: these steps mark the greatness of a nation, and the ever growing, enlightening, civilizing, and Christianizing progress are plainly seen by their greatness and their power.

What is true in these instances is true in relation to a church, which brings us to our third consideration. The church is comprised of any number of individuals for the service and worship of God; it may be regarded as a community or government—a kingdom if you please —Christ, however, is its head. The church is commanded to go forward; it must not, cannot tarry on the plain of human progress. The church has its aim and its end; it is an intelligent intellectual body; it has something in common with other intelligent agencies to do; whatever it is must be done; to accomplish which it must go forward. Is the church itself small and diminutive, it must swell and increase until its huge form can be seen like a great mountain away in the distance. The handful of corn planted must produce the wavy field, rich for the harvest. The stone cut out of the mountain must roll on and roll on until it fills the earth. The church of Christ has an interesting work to perform, and in that work there must be progress. Righteousness through it must be established, truth maintained, justice advocated, mercy pleaded; love, free, full, universal love to all, among all, contended for, with a zeal and fervor and sincerity that should know no abatement; to this end every available means must be used, every effort made; hearts and heads and hands of men must be enlisted to work out the redemption of the world; sin of every kind, cast, or color must be destroyed; against them all the church must fight, though it be against principalities and powers or spiritual wickedness in high places; every instrumentality must be seized upon to carry forward the interesting work of Christianity, civilization, redemption, reformation—revolution if need be; sin must be slain. The church must do its part, and do it well; discouragements and opposition should be no barriers, we must go forward, it is God's command. A body of godly working Christians is a sight which angels can contemplate with delight, and which God himself approves. The church must move on; from what we see it must move on, there is no encamping here, amid this battle-field of life. Men and nations and communities are heeding the command and moving forward: science is holding up its magic lamp, and by its light athwart the pathway of men and nations does she throw a broad glare to guide them in their onward course, and along its brilliant pointings is the world moving forward. The church must not lag behind lest she be pushed aside, to be passed by unnoticed and unhonored; it must go forward towards perfection in every good work; it must increase in efficiency, to benefit the world; it must be diligent and active in the pursuit of every enterprise which claims its attention and care; its efforts abroad, like its efforts at home, must be attended to; its great heart should throb for the world's salvation, and its broad arms should encircle all mankind—that is its business, its duty, and should, must be its aim; to this end the church must go forward in might and in power, put on strength and grow in grace, in knowledge, wisdom, purity, and holiness; for the church there lies the life struggle, the aim of the church. Let us of this church see to it that we move forward, that we make progress onward and upward. Our fathers went forward in their day, nobly forward; they did their duty, and they did it well; so that we now looking back upon those early times, though fifty years have rolled away and balled up all the doings of those long, long years, still can we of this later day, in view of what we now know and see, truthfully exclaim, "Well done, good and faithful servants."

What was commanded the people by the mouth of Moses was commanded by a greater than Moses to our fathers; they did go forward; they have finished their work, crossed over Jordan, and are now in Canaan and at rest. The same God, by the mouth of his son, calls upon every man and woman in this church to arise and go forward. The labors and example of our fathers show we are resting, positively snugly encamped before some Baal Zephon. My brethren, I call upon you arise; God commands you to go forward; why stop to complain, why to lament and say O Lord, look upon us in our low estate; oh, pity our condition; help us in our leanness? Moses did this very thing. God said to him, Why cryest thou to me? command the people that they go forward. And now if you would succeed, work—work while you pray; for God will help no man, nor any church that will not help themselves.

If we would insure success we must first be diligent

in what our hands find to do; we must make progress if we desire the church to prosper, and to travel in the greatness of her strength; you, my brethren, elders of this church, must walk around Zion, view her bulwarks and her towers, examine her walls, and see that all is in order, like those fathers who once occupied the position you now fill: you must repair every breach, guard every pass, secure every gate, and keep a watchful eye all around you: you are the officers of this army of our King; lead on the people; say to them Go forward, we are in an enemy's country, and our foes are pressing hard upon us; we must be up and doing; there must be less complaining and more laboring; less resting and more action; more of the vital and practical workings of Christianity than its desirings; more of the spirit's working power among us than forms and conventional formulas; in short, we must go forward in every good word and work.

And what is true of us as office bearers is true of the individual member—for we are after all members, one of another, all one in Christ, all journeying along the same pathway in life; we have the same hopes and fears, the same common enemy to fight, the same conflicts within us and without, the same aim and end in view, the same heaven in prospect, the same God to serve, and withal the same road to travel to reach our journey's end. Each member of this Zion, then, is called upon to go forward, to throw aside every weight and every burden, and the sin that doth so easily beset them, and run with patience the race that is set before them, looking at the same time to Jesus, who is the author and the finisher of our faith. The membership of a church must have a mind to work if they would see the salvation of God, in many souls being delivered from the power of sin and Satan and ushered into the marvellous light and liberty of God's children. May I call upon each one to-day to dedicate himself afresh for this desirable, nay necessary end? But how are we to do this? Can it be done alone by praying? Often this proves a delusion. Prayer of course must be used, by all means; yet are there other essentials necessary in this work; there must be an earnest, serious, and manifest interest evidenced in us all for the glory of our God, the conversion of souls, the prosperity of this church. And what evidences this? Why, the temper and spirit in which we enter and labor in it; the sacrifices we are making of our time, our means, and of our ability to do, in any way or manner, what the cause of our Redeemer demands of us. We must let our light shine before men; not our words, our professions, or our formality, but our Christian principles, Christlike to do good, and to communicate—forget not. We must be the salt of the earth; our example in life and practice must show to men that we have been with Christ and have been taught of him: this we must evidence by our daily life, daily conversation, in our intercourse with our fellow men, whether in the house or by the wayside, in the workshop, or anywhere else. We must be willing to do the will of our heavenly Father, by doing whatever our hands find to do; we must go forward; in God's work there can be no resting point. In our travels to the promised land we must go forward; God commands, it is ours to obey.

HISTORY OF THE CHURCH.

INTRODUCTORY REMARKS.

Our Saviour upon one occasion gave this command to his disciples: "Gather up the fragments that remain, let nothing be lost." Taking this command, then, in its strictest meaning, we can easily conceive that in matters of public interest it should be religiously observed.

Waiving every other subject that has a bearing upon this precious and necessary command of our Lord, we take up the church as one of the most interesting and important institutions of public concern. The Church in all of its branches, considered in their individual organizations, however widespread it may be, in whatever part of the habitable globe located, is one harmonious whole, forming a unit, a oneness, with Christ as its head. I do not think that I will be charged with any far stretched idea in making the above assertion; whoever reads the constitution which Christ has caused to be published for the government of his church on earth, must necessarily conclude with me, that his church, his visible or universal church, is one: this follows from that constitution, which is the Bible—one in its aim, one in its end, and one in its use. To gather up the history of each individual church, then, should be the aim of each disciple of the Lord Jesus, in order that its existence may be known.

If the church on earth is one, Christ being its head, there is, therefore, a common interest binding them together as a common brotherhood. As one of our poets beautifully expresses it—

"Our heavenly Father calls,
 Christ and His members one;
We the young children of his love,
 And He the first born son.
We are but several parts
 Of the same broken bread;
One body hath its several limbs,
 But Jesus is the head."

That the history of every church should be known seems equally clear from the relation they sustain to each other. That was a significant remark made by Paul to his brethren when he said: "Ye are members one of another;" how forcible and expressive is this remark—members one of another. There must be somewhat of a family tie existing between the churches. If it be so, and we cannot show why it should not, then is it clear that, as in every well-ordered family, a knowledge of each of its members is desirable and necessary, so is there reason for a knowledge of each church by every member of Christ's mystical body, the church; and however humble and weak it may be, whatever peculiar circumstance surrounds it, so much the greater reason for a knowledge of it. Upon the same principle that our sympathies are moved rather toward the weakest and most unfortunate member of a family, in like manner our interest in and anxiety for these weaker and smaller members of the Christian family should cluster around to watch over and be mindful of, simply on account of what has been already stated.

There may be many other reasons given why the knowledge of no single church of our Redeemer should be lost to the great family of Christians for the want of a history. But they are too numerous to mention in connection with the present matter we have in hand. I intend in this publication, briefly, though I trust to the satisfaction and comprehension of all who will favor me by perusing these pages, to give a history of the first African Presbyterian Church in Philadelphia, and in fact, the first established, and consequently the oldest in the United States.

In giving the history of this church, permit me, kind reader, to say, that not only the above reasons stated influenced me to write out the history of this branch of Christ's Church, but another reason induced me to undertake it. I will state it.

When Luke was about to write his Gospel, he prefaced it with these words to Theophilus: "Forasmuch as many have taken in hand to set forth in order a declaration of those things which are most surely believed among us, even as they delivered them unto us which from the beginning were eye-witnesses and ministers of the Word; it seemed good to me, also, having had perfect understanding of all things from the very first, to write unto thee, in order that thou mightest know the certainty of those things wherein thou hast been instructed."

Herein, the Evangelist was more fortunate than myself, for others had taken in hand a declaration of those things necessary to be known. In the case of the first African Church, no one had undertaken even a brief sketch of the rise of this member of the Christian family: my readers will at once see the reason why I have undertaken to write its history—that it may not be lost. Taking the command of my Saviour, then, "Gather up the fragments, let nothing be lost," I throw myself upon your indulgence, and pray my Heavenly Father to repay

2

you amply for the time you may appropriate in the perusal of these few pages, which shall be condensed as much as possible, without destroying the information necessary to be obtained, and of monopolizing too much of your time, which, for aught I know, may be more profitably engaged in this age of reading.

About the beginning of the present century, it became a subject of considerable conversation among the few colored people in Philadelphia whose preferences were Presbyterian, of raising a Presbyterian Church. This idea seemed to be general among them; but how to proceed was a matter of no small difficulty, for at the time there were very few Presbyterians in Philadelphia. There was one thing, however, that was in their favor, and it was their firmness and determination not to permit their smallness of number to prevent their making the effort; they were Christians from principle, and their hearts were in the work; their zeal and energy gave springs to their determination: with them there was no such thing as fail. The only question was, Who shall lead in the movement? Here was the true difficulty. There were true and faithful men ready to give their countenance and influence to the work, but who would sacrifice his business, his temporal prospects in life, his time, his means, his all of self? Here was the difficulty to grapple with and overcome; one that not only every new enterprise of like character, but one that the Church has ever had to contend with. Of the justness of the assertion Christians can judge; of its correctness I am sure. There were men of acknowledged ability, and other prerequisites,but it required a man who would be willing to make every sacrifice of his own time and worldly interest, to lead in the movement. For such a man they must wait patiently. It is not in the course of this brief history, to discuss the question whether it was necessary to form a separate Church for the use of colored worshippers; that is a question I take as not forming any part of a Church history proper, unless there arose some circumstance by which a separation would be forced upon the receding party. Let it suffice the reader for me to say, there was no cause of ill-treatment upon the part of existing organizations or Churches, to drive the colored membership to seek a separation; they could have remained in connection, no doubt, with the churches, and been respected as members of it. Presbyterians are remarkable for their regard to each other, without respect to distinctions—it is a characteristic of God's people. In the case, then, of raising a colored church, the prevailing opinion seemed to be, an organization of colored people where church government could be committed to, and governed by them, and that without separating from Presbyterian bodies, or alienating themselves from their fellow Christians. A church was accordingly formed, and measures adopted to supply it with preaching, which will be stated in its proper place. There seems to be a providence in these movements sometimes very remarkable, and it proved so in this case. God often "works in a mysterious way His wonders to perform"—for at this particular and interesting time, Dr. Gideon Blackburn, a Presbyterian clergyman, arrived in Philadelphia, bringing with him a body servant or slave called John Gloucester, and about whom much will be said during our notice of the history of the Church. This man was of deep piety, and well instructed in the doctrines of the Presbyterian faith. Seeing that his servant was a man of no ordinary character, that he possessed gifts and graces that evidently qualified him for the ministry, Dr. Blackburn, it will be seen in the course of this history, concluded to seek a place where Mr. Gloucester could exercise his gifts and graces in preaching the Gospel, for which he was so eminently qualified. To this end Dr. Blackburn left Tennessee, where he resided, and visited Philadelphia. What a providence is here seen; not merely a coincidence, as some would say, but a special providence. How does this visit, at this time, remind us of the question of Isaac to his Father, on Mount Moriah, "My Father, here is the altar and the wood, but where is the sacrifice?" and in keeping with our present subject is equally significant the words of Abraham, "My son, God will provide a sacrifice." In our case it was truly a special providence, and it seems clear, for God surely does watch over the interests of Zion, and are we not told "that no good thing will be withheld from them that walk uprightly." So we may safely argue that the visit of Dr. Blackburn, at this juncture, was providentially ordered, and no good reason can be adduced to the contrary. However, it was regarded as a favorable indication that God was leading in the matter, and by his own mysterious operation was producing the materials for establishing a church in Philadelphia. In order, therefore, to show more fully the leadings of the Most High toward this end, I will direct attention more particularly to the history of Mr. Gloucester.

A BRIEF REVIEW OF MR. GLOUCESTER, FIRST PASTOR OF THE FIRST AFRICAN CHURCH, PHILADELPHIA, PA.

I am led to call the attention of the reader to Mr. Gloucester's history with the Church for several reasons. Among the most prominent are: first, he is worthy of notice; another is, he was chosen by the Most High, through His Church, to lead this people; one other is, that considering his labors in the church, it necessarily becomes interesting; the last I shall offer is the exhortation of Paul, "Remember them which have the rule over you, who have spoken unto you the Word of God."

The first intimation had of Mr. Gloucester was derived from the minutes of the Presbytery of Union, Synod of Tennessee, to the General Assembly, in 1807, presented to that body by the Committee of Overtures, requesting advice in relation to the licensure of Mr. John Gloucester. The case was handed over to a committee appointed by the General Assembly, consisting of Messrs. Clark, Miller, and Samuel Brown, with instructions to report as early as possible. After due time the Committee made the following report:—

"*Whereas*, From the communication of the Presbytery of Union, it appears that John Gloucester has been for some time under the care of the Presbytery of Union, that in the opinion of Presbytery he possesses promising talents and eminent piety; that he has been for several years engaged in the study of literature and theology, but has not yet obtained all the literary qualifications required in candidates for licensure, and if he were licensed there is much reason to believe he might be highly useful in preaching the Gospel among his own people; and *Whereas*, said Presbytery requests the advice of the General Assembly, therefore

"*Resolved*, That the General Assembly, considering the circumstances of the particular case, viz., the evidence of unusual talents, discretion, and piety, possessed by John Gloucester, the good reason there is to believe that he may be highly useful in preaching the Gospel among people of his own color, and the various difficulties likely to attend a further delay in proceeding in this case, the General Assembly did and hereby do authorize the Presbytery of Philadelphia to consider the case of John Gloucester, and if they think proper, to license him to preach the Gospel." *Extr. Min.* 1807, pp. 381, 387.

The communication from the Presbytery of Union (Tennessee), that elicited the above action of the General Assembly, as deduced from the resolution of the General Assembly, may not be unimportant, as it shows clearly the reasonableness of the action of the Assembly under the circumstances, and will go far to recommend to the favorable notice of the general reader, the character of Mr. Gloucester.

It will not be out of place here, to bring before the reader the action of the Philadelphia Presbytery, sitting in the second Presbyterian Church, in the City of Philadelphia, July 7, 1807, the following members of Presbytery being present: Dr. Wm. Tennant, Archibald Alexander, George C. Potts, Jacob T. Janeway, and James P. Wilson, Ministers; Messrs. Benjamin Weeks, Hugh Henry, and John Harris, Elders. The Presbytery having ascertained that this meeting was agreeable to constitutional rules, summoned with a view to take into consideration the case of John Gloucester, referred to them by the last General Assembly, chose Mr. Alexander for Moderator, and Mr. Janeway for Clerk.

The case was then taken into consideration, when, after reading the document laid before the Presbytery relative to Mr. Gloucester, and having maturely deliberated on the circumstances in his case, the Presbytery were of opinion that as he has been educated under care of the Presbytery of Union, and as they are fully competent to decide on his case, and will be able to decide with more understanding than this Presbytery could without having more time than his circumstances will allow, it was, on motion, *Resolved*, Not to take said John Gloucester on trial with a view to licensure. Ordered, that the stated clerk furnish Mr. Gloucester with a copy of the above minute.

This seeming discouragement did not, however, cool the ardor of Mr. Gloucester's zeal, or determination to labor for the salvation of souls. He understood the motive of this presbyterial course was to put the case where it properly belonged, and that in view of all the facts in his peculiar case, it was the proper course. He at once yielded to the decision of Presbytery, and returned to Tennessee, within the bounds of his Presbytery, and awaited their action. Here we may gather a reflection, and at once decide that there was an excellent spirit in the man; there was a patience and resignation that would grace the character of any professing Christian.

It will be perceived that the action of the Philadelphia Presbytery was on July 7, 1807, and on April 16, 1811, the Philadelphia Presbytery, sitting in Philadelphia, in the Second Presbyterian Church, Dr. Alexander, Moderator, we obtain the following information:—

"The testimonials of Rev. John Gloucester were exhibited to Presbytery, and ordered to be recorded on the minutes, as follows:—

"Extract of a minute of the Presbytery of Union (Tennessee), Baker's Creek, April 30, 1810.—Immediately after the ordination sermon, Mr. Gloucester having satisfactorily answered the questions usually put to candidates on such occasions, the Presbytery proceeded to set apart, and did solemnly ordain the said John Gloucester, by prayer and the laying on of the hands of the Presbytery. The right hand of fellowship being duly given, and he solemnly charged to the faithful discharge of his duty, he was ordered as soon as possible to repair to the City of Philadelphia, and directed to join the Presbytery of that city, whereby he is recommended as a man of fair morals and upright conduct, both as a man, a Christian, and a minister, and is recommended to the faithful care and Christian attention of the Presbytery of Philadelphia.

GIDEON BLACKBURN, *Moderator*.
JOSEPH B. LAPSLEY, *Clerk*.

"Dated May 1st, 1810."

Whereupon, the Presbytery of Philadelphia

Resolved, That Mr. Gloucester be and he is hereby received as a member of this Presbytery.

It is not to be understood that, during this time, the interesting effort of organizing the church was in any way abated or suffered to flag for the want of care or attention from friends favorable to the movement. In the proper place I shall show that during the time that intervened between the action of the two Presbyteries and the ordination of Mr. Gloucester, he not only labored himself, assisted by the ministers of the Presbytery, but that the infant church was raised, organized, and progressing very encouragingly. I make this digression from the regular record of proceeding in the course of a history, from the fact that this case of Mr. Gloucester, from its peculiarity, warrants it. His peculiar condition prevents me from a regularity in recording much of his history, and the state of things at that early time in relation to him, prevented the Presbyteries from acting as they would in ordinary cases coming before them; hence the seeming discrepancies that appear in the narrative. In view of keeping this record clear, I must refer back to Mr. Gloucester's case from the time that it was first brought before the General Assembly, in 1807, and sitting, as I have shown, in Lexington, Kentucky.

In several of the general assemblies it was a matter of considerable interest to many of the members as it regards the religious training of colored people; it was most generally conceded that it should be done through missionary effort. To this end, a Mr. John Chavis, a colored man, was brought to the notice of the assembly, and recommended as a man of good literary acquirements; he was subsequently received, licensed, and ordained. This was in the year 1801. (*Gen. Assembly Digest*, page 206.) Mr. Alexander sought to obtain his service for Philadelphia, but failed. Lexington claimed and obtained his service to labor within their bounds.

The General Assembly sitting in Lexington, Kentucky, in 1807, John Gloucester was recommended to the Assembly, by the Presbytery of Union Synod of Tennessee, as a candidate for licensure to labor as a missionary among colored people. Dr. Alexander at once seized upon the circumstance as a favorable opportunity of securing the services of Mr. Gloucester in forwarding and carrying out his long cherished desire of raising up a church in Philadelphia. He lost no time in communicating with Dr. Blackburn, the owner of Mr. Gloucester, who at once acceded to the proposal, and consented that Mr. Gloucester should, as the incipient step to his future labors, visit Philadelphia as soon as possible.

Accordingly, Dr. Blackburn, attended by Mr. Gloucester, arrived in Philadelphia immediately after the rise of the General Assembly. Drs. Alexander and Green were not long arriving at a conclusion in view of so favorable an opportunity.

As the Evangelical Society (which will be noticed more particularly hereafter) had taken, or adopted measures for organizing the colored people into a Presbyterian Church, Dr. Alexander proposed to Dr. Blackburn, that Mr. Gloucester be employed by the Evangelical Society to labor as a missionary among the colored people. I am credibly informed by a gentleman conversant with the facts, and who is one of the very few remaining who remember the doings of those early times, that Drs. Green, Janeway, Potts, and Alexander, together with Messrs. McMullin, Markoe, and Ralston, joined their earnest importunities in favor of obtaining the services of Mr. Gloucester. To these importunities Dr. Blackburn yielded, relinquishing, on his part, all pay or emolument from any labor that Mr. Gloucester might perform as a missionary among the people, and freeing him at the same time from "any service or labor which to him (Dr. Blackburn) may be due." Mr. Gloucester was not long in Philadelphia before a wide door was opened unto him for preaching the Word of life to many anxious people; he, too, was not long deciding upon his proper course of action; he saw the field white for the harvest, and few laborers therein; looking to God, he stripped himself for the work, and cheerfully entered upon his duties. He first commenced his missionary efforts by preaching in private houses; but such were the number of people that attended his ministry, that in a very short time no private house could be found to contain the people that flocked to hear him expound God's Word. It was very evident that the time had come when it must be said This place is too narrow for us.

The result of this success led to street preaching. He notified the people that, at least in clear weather, he should preach at the corner of Seventh and Shippen Streets; and, when the weather was not favorable, he had obtained the use of a school-house near by. To these places his hearers resorted, and there each consecutive Sabbath, this devoted servant of God preached the Gospel to a large number of serious hearers. Through these meetings this branch of Christ's Church was gathered, and, from the most reliable information derived from one who was interested in raising this church, did Drs. Alexander and Green, assisted by other friends of the cause, in the latter part of May, 1807, organize this church to be known and distinguished as the First African Presbyterian Church, and as such was received by the Assembly's Committee on Missions, and, as in other cases, provision made and provided accordingly.

From this time, Mr. Gloucester had to labor almost alone in this arduous work. Nor are we to understand that he was without opposition—it would be an anomaly in Christian enterprise—sectarian bigotry is the same bitter, malignant enemy to all that is not of its cast, and knows no change. Like its father, the devil, it goes about, seeking whom it may devour. And not only in that particular respect, but, as it were, he had principalities and powers, and spiritual wickedness in high places to contend against. There were influences brought to bear directly upon him that were intended to crush in the bud the least appearance of establishing a Presbyterian church. It can be seen that Mr. Gloucester did not have a free wind and full tide to waft him gently onwards; but otherwise, there were those around him who professedly were friendly, and seemingly much interested in his welfare, but whose real designs were selfish and mean, and who persuaded him that it was a waste of time for him to attempt, in Philadelphia, to raise a Presbyterian church, that the people in heart were Methodist, and would finally all be received into Methodist churches.

With many, the doctrines of the Presbyterian Church were in bad odor, and they failed not to make capital of it; others were "careful for none of these things." So it can be perceived that it required a man of no ordinary nerve and large share of the grace of God in his heart to battle with and overcome these opposing forces. Mr. Gloucester was the man for the occasion and the time; opposition could never deter him from duty; if God was for him, he cared not who was against him; in Christ lay all his strength and hope of success. Naturally, he was of a strong mind, as well as of stout, athletic frame, with a voice the deep tones of which fell powerfully on the ear—he preached the Word. He was also a very sweet singer, and it is said of him that such was the melody and rich tones of his voice that, whenever he sang, a volume of music would roll from his mouth, charming and enchaining, as by a spell, the listening audience, and holding them in sweet suspense until he would cease to sing, when the spell would be broken and the people relieved, determined upon the first occasion to return and enjoy the labors of this devoted man as he broke unto them the bread of life, and sang again another of those songs of Zion. In prayer he was mighty; such was the fervor and energy, such his wrestling when engaged, that souls have fallen under its power, deeply convicted of sin. An anecdote is related of him, soon after his arrival in Philadelphia, that ought not to be lost. I will take this opportunity of relating it:—

Mr. Gloucester boarded with a man whose name was Jacob Craig, and whose wife was a very pious woman, and who attended the ministry of Mr. Gloucester in his open air preaching. Mr. Craig was a sailmaker by occupation, but at the same time was a great fiddler, and being such, was a source of unhappiness to his wife. After his daily toil was over, and Mr. Jacob Craig became somewhat rested, he would invariably wile away the evening by playing his fiddle, to the annoyance of his wife. Jacob was not like Jacob of old; he knew more of his fiddle than of his God, and perhaps loved it more. Things went on this way until Mr. Gloucester proposed to Sister Craig that they should hold a series of prayer meetings at her house. It was accepted, and Mr. Jacob Craig was duly informed. At first he objected, but his wife, true as steel to her purpose and faithful to her God, pressed her cause so earnestly to her husband that he consented, determined, however, to hire a room adjoining the prayer meeting, and so annoy them by continuing to play his fiddle. This he put into practice, so that whilst there was praying in one apartment, there was Mr. Craig fiddling in the other. Here there was a difficulty as to who should yield in this. Mr. Gloucester's advice was sought. He replied, that for his part he was contented to remain where he was; it was an open field and a fair fight, and that was all he asked. From that decision there was no appeal—God approved it. In a few nights after, there was no sound of a fiddle heard. A few evenings after, Mr. Jacob Craig came home and attended, for the first time, the prayer meeting; he had given up the room and stopped playing; a very little while after he was seen to weep, then heard to exclaim: "God have mercy on me, a poor miserable man." The battle was fought—the prize was won; the Lord had mercy on the man—he was converted, and afterwards set apart as an elder in Seventh Street Church, under Mr. Gloucester, through whose instrumentality he was brought into the fold of Christ, and into the marvellous light and liberty of His children, and continued in the Church a pious, devoted, and faithful Christian until the day of his death, and we hope has entered into that rest that remains for the people of God.

Of Mr. Gloucester's early history very little is known; this is not surprising, considering the peculiarity of his condition, being once a slave, but having been converted to God under the preaching of Dr. Blackburn, and evidencing after that such piety and devotion, that Dr. Blackburn, struck with the excellency of the man, and the intelligence of one in his condition, he was induced to purchase him, it is said, and we have every reason to believe the assertion true, that Dr. Blackburn took particular pains to educate Mr. Gloucester, and so prepare and qualify him as a minister of the Gospel. In this respect Dr. Blackburn deserves all credit, for Mr. Gloucester was indeed a "workman that needed not to be ashamed," for he knew well how to divide the Word of life, giving to each his portion in due season. This no doubt accounts for the number of persons that waited or attended upon his ministry—and it is a fact that his deep piety and earnest devotion to his calling made him very many friends from among the rich and influential citizens of Philadelphia; he not only had the warm and abiding friendship of such men as Drs. Alexander, Green, Janeway and Potts, and the members of the Presbyterian churches then in Philadelphia, but Dr. Rush, the world-wide known philanthropist of Philadelphia, was almost a regular attendant wherever he preached, and many other citizens of influence were frequent visitors upon his stated ministry. Messrs. McMullin, Markoe, Ralston, Jenkins, Sawyer, and lady, encouraged his heart and strengthened his hands, and by their presence and support under God lightened his labors and cheered him in his duties. The various Presbyterian churches in the city were also interested in his favor, and took a deep interest in his efforts to raise this church.

Mr. Gloucester was also diligent in his calling, and of fervent spirit—necessary qualities for a minister of

Jesus, who, like his master, would leave his footprints on time, and his impressions on the world—the laborer in the field must work if he would glean the harvest—he must, like the racer, stretch every nerve to reach the goal if he would win the prize and take the crown—so thought this humble servant of the Most High. He lost no time whatever; to wear out was his motto, to rust out never. He knew, as he often said, his days were few, and he would spend them to the best advantage and to the glory of his God. He had a presentiment that his day was well spent, and the night of his death was at hand. Thus we find him only living to live again in regions of light, life, and immortality beyond this vale of tears, this land of suffering and toil. It is said by one of the remaining few left from those long years—long fled in the past, that each succeeding Sabbath as early as 6 o'clock in the morning would Mr. Gloucester come and stand at the corner of Seventh and Shippen Sts., and there, by a hymn of praise which few could sing so sweetly as he, draw together a large concourse of people; then, taking advantage of the circumstance, would take some passage of Scripture and preach the Word of life to the people; and such was the moral influence acting upon the minds of the persons keeping dram shops in the neighborhood for the sale of that soul and body destroying agent, ardent spirits, that they would not open their groggeries until meeting, as they called it, was over, and Mr. Gloucester retired. I do not presume too much when I say that from the time he first commenced his labors in Philadelphia to the time when that fell destroyer of ministers, consumption, laid hold upon his vitals, and which terminated his useful life on the 2d May, in the year 1822, he labored with the same zeal and diligence as made him the ever faithful pastor. As it regarded his manner of preaching it was remarkable. He abounded in anecdotes, for he was a close observer of everything that was transpiring around him, and having travelled extensively and gathered much information therefrom, he could illustrate his subjects to the comprehension of all classes of his hearers from things seen, and, like his great teacher the Lord Jesus, whose life and example he sought to imitate, he had the peculiar faculty of drawing abundantly from the book of nature a variety of subjects, and adapting and applying them to some text of Scripture so easily comprehended as to give a point and edge to his subject that convinced and cut into the consciences of sinners, convincing them of the truth of God's Word. His manner was bold, his voice clear and loud. In his invitations to the trembling mourner and earnest inquirer he was interestingly mild and inviting; but to the careless sinner, in his denunciations he was terrible. The flashes of his eye, in contrast with his tall, commanding and noble figure, his gestures at the same time giving a cast to his earnestness of soul, at once struck and awed the most wayward and inconsiderate; it has been said of him "he was wise to win souls."

Mr. Gloucester was not only a faithful man in his pulpit, but out of it; he visited extensively among his people, not only among his own followers or members, but wherever he could find access. The poor, the lowly, the outcast found in him an adviser, a friend. In this he was the reformer as well as the Gospel minister. He became, so to speak, all things unto all men, that by all means he might save some. He had the peculiar gift of entering into the feelings of the people. If he saw anything wrong among the families he visited, in their domestic matters

—whether it was in person for the want of care and attention to cleanliness—he never failed to impress upon them how necessary, in order to health and respectability, this necessary observance. If they were careless of their children, not training them properly and taking care to keep them in becoming attire, and sending them to school regularly and punctually to time, he would never leave that house until he had given a lecture upon parental duties to children; and so wherever he went he instructed the people on moral training, and preached to them the Gospel of the Son of God. "In labors therefore he was abundant." I will take occasion here to remark that Mr. Gloucester during his life, and in the discharge of his pastoral duties over the Church, kept a day school for the education of children, and in which department of labor he took considerable delight. It was not to him the least interesting part of his duties, for he was fond of children, a peculiarity by no means discreditable to him. From it in connection with the Sabbath school a nursery was in training wherein was to be reared trees of righteousness that in God's own time were to bloom in the garden of the Lord, and be established in the mountains of his house.

What an auxiliary, also, to the Sabbath School. Many now living can attest, that through this school they were brought under the direct training of the minister. So it can be perceived, in this case, that being taught each day, they became habituated to his instructions, in his manner and mode; thus, in a large majority of cases, pupils learn to reverence and honor the teacher. By this course there is laid up in the youthful mind the buddings of future confidence and respect, that time nor influence can never completely eradicate, but will more or less exert a beneficial control over the conduct of the mature man ; and besides this, the early impressions of youth linger around the memory, and delight to cluster in old age the memories of its youth ; hence our parental love, our strong affection for early friends, and so far are we influenced by it, that even inanimate objects have a degree of importance and regard attached to them ; whether it be a stone by the wayside, or an old oak tree, are memory's treasures dear and precious. For our Christian teachers this is remarkably true, children ever retain for their instructors a regard little short of parental affection; hence the veneration that the young entertained for Mr. Gloucester.

I once before intimated, that during Mr. Gloucester's ministry, he was not without his troubles. I will take the occasion now, however, to say that he had the peculiar trait or tact of restraining within bounds the turbulent dispositions of men, controlling within proper limits those unnatural flashes that sometimes gleam out of religious assemblies in murmurings and complaints. In this peculiar quality he was fortunate. His situation was a trying one, particularly when we consider that his congregation was a mixed one, made up of some who had come from other churches, each holding more or less peculiar views of his own, others from a conviction of duty to God and the exceeding sinfulness of sin ; these were from the world, snatched from the very jaws of the lion ; still they were unacquainted with government, and had to be broken in to the rule and order of the church. In a new organization such as the one I am now treating on, there cannot be much wonder that discordant elements among them should exist, and it can be seen, also, that no small amount of wisdom and prudence, as well as grace, is required to govern and guide a congregation thus constituted; still it is true, that if men would consult God's will and word, more than they do their own predilections and passions, none of these things could possibly exist.

Another view of Mr. Gloucester's history may not be uninteresting, upon which I will direct attention. Mr. Gloucester had considerable labor to undergo during his brief ministerial career: not only the care and burden of the Church, not only the hopes of the people confiding in him filled his heart and soul with much anxiety, but there was his wife and four children in slavery; it was not possible for him to rest quiet and at ease under such a circumstance as that! O no, these must be redeemed from bondage, and hence we account for the reason why it was that he was so often absent from his Church and Presbytery.

He travelled extensively in the States of the Union, in nearly every principal city north and south, raising collections or contributions in order to purchase the freedom of his family, and he met with kind friends who afforded him every assistance, and so near his heart did this matter lie, and to such an extent did it excite him, that when he found that all the means necessary for the redemption of his wife and children could not be obtained in the United States, he crossed the ocean and landed in England, and plead for money to buy his family. He was successful, and returned to America, purchased them, rejoiced to have them free, to call them his, to see them settled in Philadelphia, happy and cheerful, and then to give himself again to the labors of the ministry in building up the church: surely, like the great Apostle to the Gentiles, "in labors he was abundant," and in comparison to many ministers, he "labored more abundantly than they." Contemplating him from this standpoint, I might ask did he not deserve the respect as well as sympathy of every Christian and enlightened heart?—and he possessed it, and I am pleased to record that many were the testimonials he received from such. Among the many that might be inserted in this biography of him, I will take the liberty of asserting, that the success attending his efforts to obtain the freedom of his family, in Europe and the United States, is unmistakable proof of a deep and abiding sympathy in his favor.

In closing this brief history of Mr. Gloucester, I must not permit to escape the notice of an instance of deep concern felt for him by a lady of Philadelphia, a member of the Society of Friends, and which, if duly considered, will go very far to show that his labors were not only approved, but a decided mark was made on the public mind, through the course pursued by him in his instructions to his people. The letter herein inserted is from Mrs. Grace Douglass, the wife of Mr. Robert Douglass, one of the original founders of the Church so frequently alluded to in this history. The letter was written to Rev. John Gloucester when in Europe.

PHILADELPHIA, Feb. 28th, 1819.

DEAR FRIEND: Being in meeting this morning, I felt a little exercised that I might be useful in promoting the glory of our Master and the good of my fellow-creatures. The professing part of your congregation in particular, seemed to be upon my mind, and Oh, thought I, if they would be persuaded to try a little of my experience it might do them good in a temporal way, as I do not feel qualified in spiritual things. It has been said by our enemies among the whites, that it is doing us harm to set us free: we cannot, say they, maintain ourselves decently and respectably. Some of them must manage for us. To prove which, they bid us look around and see the many poor distressed objects of our color with which this city abounds, where we have every encouragement to do well for ourselves, overlooking the manner in which most of us have been brought up. Very many, in great families where they live on the best, dress in the finest and most fashionable clothing. They have had everything provided for the body without their thought or care. Man being an imitative animal, of course they carry these customs into their own families. They work hard, therefore they have money to spend, and must enjoy it in the way they have seen others do. And they are apt, too, to think they have a right to do so, as they have *worked* for it. When I was first married I found myself precisely in this way. We had our parties and tea-drinkings; we must have the best wine and the best cake; our friends had it and we must give them the same they gave us, or be considered mean. But when it pleased the Lord to open my eyes, these things became a burden to me. I remembered He had said "When thou makest a feast call in the poor, the lame and the blind, those who cannot bid thee again." When I became more engaged to follow Christ I remembered that when on earth, he went about doing good. I thought I would assist the poor too if I had the means some people had, but I have no more than I want myself; how can *I* help the poor? Then it occurred to me that Christ lived a self-denying life, and I began to think how I might deny myself, take up the cross and follow him, when dress presented itself to my view. Now a pair of morocco shoes cost one dollar and 50 cts.: a pair of leather will do just as well, and I shall have 50 cts. for the poor. A fine muslin dress costs five dollars: I can buy a very good calico one for three, and have two dollars to spare. I reasoned in this manner till my dress was reduced to the standard which you see. I wore a plain straw bonnet with a white ribbon. The ribbon often soiled and required to be changed. I thought if I wore a plain silk one the strings will last as long as the bonnet, and here will be something saved.

These things were very trifling in themselves, but oh! the peace of mind and the liberty I gained by it more than doubly compensated me for the mortification I at first endured in seeing others who could not afford it so well, better dressed than myself. I could now go to meeting let the weather be as it would, I was not afraid of spoiling my shoes or any part of my dress. I no longer felt disturbed as to whether my appearance was better than my neighbor or not, and I always had something for the poor.

Now, dear friend, if you please, read this in one of your select meetings to those dear professing friends of yours, and beg them to try my plan for one year, and I think they cannot fail to be much benefited by it.

I remain your friend with
much regard,
GRACE DOUGLASS.

The design of Mrs. Douglass becomes very evident when we reflect upon all the circumstances by which Mr. Gloucester and his people were surrounded, for it must be observed that their labors to establish and build up the Church, to redeem from bondage his family, required no small amount of anxiety on their part; but the assistance of kind friends—whether it be in a pecuniary way, or which, in some cases, may be as valuable—the counsel and suggestions of those whose mature judgment and observation qualify them to render advice wholesome and good. In this instance, surely, it was a very opportune time in this Christian lady to interpose her advice, gathered from close observation of things around her as they existed. Evidently it was a time to retrench every indulgence, whether of dress, eating, pleasures of any kind, save those where some practical good would ensue, in favor of their efforts. Of Mr. Gloucester's subsequent labors in the Church, I have not much to record. His failing health, which for some time gave unmistakable evidence that his day of pilgrimage was wellnigh spent, gave no small uneasiness to his flock and anxiety to friends. Consumption had settled fairly upon him, and making a wreck of the once strong man. It was a heart-rending sight to behold the faithful venerable pastor, wasting away gradually but surely for the tomb; it was crushing to behold him, in the strength of manhood, weakened and wasted away by the destroyer, and no possibility of escape. To him, however, it was a very little matter to decay and die; but his anxiety lay in another direction—it was towards his Church—the people, the object of all his anxieties, these lay near his heart; to them, during the latter part of his life, he gave the remaining energies of his mind, without much regard to anything else; hence his petition to his presbytery on the 27th June, 1820, stating his weakened condition and failing health, and requesting supplies for the pulpit, and also, knowing that the day of his stay on earth was wellnigh over, why, one year before he died, he took the occasion to address a letter to presbytery, dated April 18, 1821, recommending his son Jeremiah as a candidate for the Gospel ministry. Previous to this, however, Mr. Gloucester, through the concurrence of the Church, had brought forward Samuel Cornish and Benjamin Hughes to presbytery, to be received under their care as candidates for the ministry; and, from what I have gathered from the Minutes of Presbytery, these young men sustained themselves creditably in the parts of trial assigned them by presbytery, from time to time as they were examined. In this, also, Mr. Gloucester's qualities for perception were conspicuous. It will be perceived that his vision was not circumscribed within the narrow limits of his own immediate wants or interests; he was, as I have once before stated, a man of extensive observation; he threw his furtive glance far away into the future, and contemplated the Presbyterian Church, in the States of the Union, rising in the distance as in miniature, and still later looming up in greater magnitude, until he fully recognized its swelling proportions, from every point of view, spreading out and extending itself far and wide. Hence, as can easily be perceived, he took the timely precaution to have prepared the proper material in these young candidates for the ministry, in due time to supply the growing wants of these rising churches; and it is mainly to him and to this First African Presbyterian Church that the now respectable number of Presbyterian churches in this land are supplied with ministers.

During the fifteen years of Mr. Gloucester's ministry,

the Church increased rapidly in numbers—this can be seen from the increase reckoning from the number of those admitted to the Communion of the Lord's table immediately after the people were organized into a church—the number admitted on the occasion being twenty-two; at the time of his death they numbered over three hundred communicant members—surely this was an encouraging feature of his labors.

There were, during his ministry, six elders in the Church, to wit: Messrs. James Prosser, Cato Freeman, Quammany Clarkson, Peter McNeal, Jacob Craig, and Francis Webb. Of this band of faithful men, every one of them have passed away—for God took them—only one remains, and that one is Mr. James Prosser, the first acting elder appointed by the people and pastor at the rise of the Church; and, is it not also a singular fact that of the ministers of the Presbytery who took an interest in the rise and organization of the Church, consisting of Rev'ds Ashbel Green, Archibald Alexander, J. Janeway, and George C. Potts, not one remain until this day except Dr. Jacob J. Janeway: all the rest, we hope, have entered into that rest that remains for the people of God. And I add further, that of the elders that were engaged in this interesting work, consisting of Messrs. McMullin, Markoe, Nassau, Ralston, and Capt. Moore, but one remains alive now to tell us of the struggles of that early time, and that one is Mr. William Nassau; all the others "do rest from their labors, and their works do follow them," and how interesting must it be to these aged brethren to wander back in their contemplations to these early days, and draw to their minds the companions of their youth—the veteran followers of Jesus—who so devotedly gave themselves to the Lord, and labored so earnestly in behalf of this Church.

It pleased the great Head of the Church to remove Mr. Gloucester from his earthly toils and labors, on the 2d day of May, 1822, in the 46th year of his age. This solemn event was expected, from the known nature of his disease, and though it shrouded the hearts of his people and friends in mourning and sorrow, still they were prepared for the sad announcement; in fact, he himself, though feeble and weak, daily exhorted them to resignation to the will of God. I need not inform the reader of the gloom that his death cast over the community where he was known, and he was extensively known to the religious community; they all felt that not only a great man had fallen that day in Israel, but a father, a light in the church, a shining light was extinguished.

His death was a peaceful one, full of hope; it might, perhaps, more properly be said that he fell asleep in Jesus. Could it be otherwise? His life was Christ-like, that was his life to be like Christ; for this he lived, for this he labored. I close the life of this devoted servant of God by a remark or two. That there were other colored men in Philadelphia laboring for the religious elevation of their people, is known, but if there ever was a man in Philadelphia of Mr. Gloucester's position, whose upright and Christian walk and general character, considered from every point of view, that won for him the respect and esteem of the great and good men of his day, that man was Mr. Gloucester.

His Christianity knew no partiality—it was universal, embracing all mankind—there was a sacred feeling embedded in his devoted heart towards all God's children, that was not confined to denominational distinctions, much less sectarian bigotry: his constant teachings to his flock were founded on God's universal law to man, "Love God, and your neighbor as yourself." This universal law he carried out in his life and practice; this he handed down to posterity, and this law is to this day observed by his church, and though for the maintenance of it the church be censured and proscribed by those who would have them violate that universal law of the Most High, yet are they content to follow in the footsteps of their leader in the maintenance of it, until they shall see some good reason why they should, by any act of theirs, set up a separate and distinct organization, bounded by a distinction not at all warranted in God's Word, nor yet even in a sound morality. Acknowledged now, as in the days of Mr. Gloucester, as one of the family of Presbyterians, this old church is content to abide by the landmarks laid down by the Apostles, and which we know is the only true principle taught by the Saviour, the opinions of other persons to the contrary notwithstanding.

THE RISE OF THE CHURCH, AND THE INSTRUMENTALITY BY WHICH IT WAS ACCOMPLISHED.

I am under obligation to Mr. William Nassau, one of the few surviving Christian men now alive of that constellation of godly men who devoted their time and energies in rearing the Church, for much of the information herein recorded. Mr. Nassau was an elder of the church of which Dr. Alexander was pastor, at the time the effort was made to establish the church. Also, to Mr. James Prosser, the first elder elected under Mr. Gloucester, and the only one living at present among the colored elders that were engaged in the enterprise; and to Mr. Samuel

Bass, who, though not one of the original actors in the work, yet may be regarded as one of the Fathers of the Church, as he is one of the three survivors of that early time who joined the church whilst yet in its infancy: all the rest have departed this life, and I trust have joined the Church triumphant above, and enjoy rest from their labors.

In the year 1806 Rev. Archibald Alexander, D. D., universally known as a ripe scholar and devoted servant to the cause of his Saviour, was Pastor of the Third Presbyterian Church in Philadelphia. About this time he recommended to his Christian brethren the formation of an Institution in the city, to be comprised of all persons desirous of advancing the interests of Christianity, and in order to carry out the object to a practical purpose, an institution was organized subsequently known as the "Evangelical Society of Philadelphia."

At first but eight or nine persons responded to the recommendation, and from this small number a very important institution was established, which, under the approbation of the Most High, proved instrumental in doing much good. But a short time had elapsed before it was seen that this Society would be as a right arm to the Presbyterian churches in the city and its vicinity; thereupon a large increase of ministers and laymen gave their hearts and their influence to the objects of the Society, which insured success.

At this time there were but four Presbyterian churches in the city, and if documents of that early date can be relied upon, there were not over one thousand communicant members of the Presbyterian Church in all the city, yet it was no bar to the godly few to labor for God. In this Dr. Alexander took the lead. He recommended that the members of the Evangelical Society form themselves into companies, and that each company hold prayer meetings as best suited them as to time and place; to gather children wherever they could be obtained, form them into classes, teach them the truths of the Bible, assist them in every possible way by storing their minds with useful Christian instruction, such as committing to memory passages of Scripture, selections of hymns, and sacred poetry. In this true labor of love they were successful, and from what has been known to result from this effort, we assume not too much when we say that it was the future in embryo of the Presbyterian churches in the city, and in many places contiguous to it, and from which many precious jewels of God have been brought into the fold of Christ, who in their day were to fill up the waste places in Zion, and, like their fathers, labor diligently in the vineyard of the Lord.

Among the objects brought before the Society by Dr. Alexander, was the religious training of the colored people. He pointed to them as special subjects of attention from the Society. He regarded this class of the community with deep interest. Surely it was Godlike in him to look after these sheep of the house of Israel; it was a consideration worthy of him, and it was one toward which he gave his powerful influence, and lent the powers of his giant intellect. Considering the times and the circumstances that then surrounded the colored people, I would say it was a great undertaking; but Dr. Alexander was a great man. He did not stop "to confer with flesh and blood" upon the matter; he saw his duty plain, and knowing it, he did it. His God and his own large heart sustained him in his effort. From his known interest toward the welfare of the colored people, Dr. Alexander has earned for himself the name of a Christian philanthropist. Our church honors him as its patron and advocate—indeed, as its founder—and he will ever live in their memories as one of the noblest specimens of the Creator's production of a Christian and gentleman. I must by no means omit other gentlemen who took similar views and entertained kindred feelings with Dr. Alexander, in behalf of the colored people. Prominently with him were Rev. Ashbel Green, D. D., who, to the latest period of his life, always regarded this African Church (whose history I am recording) with much interest, as will be seen when I come to treat more particularly upon it. Dr. J. Janeway, likewise, with Rev. George Potts, regarded the recommendation and gave it their sanction. Of the laity, Messrs. McMullin, Ralston, Markoe, and Nassau, accorded to the views of Dr. Alexander, and were not slack in their efforts to advance the measure; and I am happy to record among the advocates of our welfare, gentlemen from other bodies of Christians. Messrs. Jenkins and Sawyer, of the Baptist Church, and Dr. Benjamin Rush, of the Society of Friends, gave their influence and support to it; in fact, with but a very few exceptions, not by any means necessary now particularly to designate, all the churches over which Drs. Alexander, Green, Janeway, and Potts were pastors, encouraged them in the affair and strengthened their hands—particularly the ladies of the first, second, third and fourth Presbyterian Churches: it would prove an anomaly in this case were it otherwise, for they are ever foremost in every good work.

Whilst this subject was under consideration before the Evangelical Society, and they were discussing the subject of forming in Philadelphia a colored Presbyterian congregation, Dr. Gideon Blackburn, a Presbyterian minister from Tennessee, arrived in the city with his body servant or slave John Gloucester, as I have once before shown. In regard, however, to this Church of colored people, here was a favorable indication, to say the least of it, and the friends of the movement did not intend that it should slip by them without an effort to secure it. They were determined to do something for the religious benefit of the people. In this they were of one mind and heart; is it cause for wonder that they were successful in securing from Dr. Blackburn the services of Mr. Gloucester for this interesting field of labor? nay, in union there is strength, is a truth clear as it is trite. The reader will pardon me for calling attention to another fact not perhaps generally known in order to show that Dr. Alexander and the friends that acted with him in seeking to raise a Presbyterian congregation among colored people pursued a justifiable course.

At this time (1806) Philadelphia contained a numerous colored population.

Among this vast body of people at this time there were in all the city and vicinity for miles but one Episcopal church, under the rectorship of the Rev. Absalom Jones, a colored Episcopal clergyman; and I will take this occasion of saying that Mr. Jones was ever the firm and abiding friend of Mr. Gloucester. That church contained a membership of about one hundred and fifty persons. Bethel and Zoar Churches, under the Methodist Episcopal Church, contained between them about one thousand members, making in all about eleven hundred and fifty colored communicant members.

There were no other colored churches of other denominations. It can be seen at a glance that to raise up and establish a Presbyterian Church in the city was a movement as judicious as necessary, and wise as desirable; thus we may conceive them laboring to this end. In the brief notice I have taken of Mr. Gloucester and of his labors I called attention to the method at first adopted of gathering up the people, by preaching and holding prayer meetings in private houses, and often in the street. These meetings, or, as they were more properly regarded, religious gatherings, were not without interest, and to a considerable extent successful. Many who were heretofore careless of their souls' spiritual well-being were alarmed, and convicted under Mr. Gloucester's preaching; others were converted unto God under the hammer of the Word as it fell from his lips. Not a few connected with other churches were struck with the intelligence of the man, and the power of his preaching, the unction that attended his appeals, and the ability with which he handled his subject, so that in a comparatively short time, taking everything into consideration, it became very evident that a favorable impression upon the minds of the people was being made. The large number of persons that attended upon his stated ministry, whether in the house, or in his open-air meetings—the deep attention paid to his discourse as being delivered, together with the healthy influence he was creating all around him — are so many points in proof that he was gaining rapidly, into the good graces of the community, and working himself into the affections of not a few. An offer was made, and a very strong inducement held out to Mr. Gloucester to relinquish his efforts of raising a

Presbyterian Colored Church, and give the weight of his influence, the energies of his mind in another direction, and ample provision, &c., should be afforded him ; but Mr. Gloucester was a man who could neither be bought nor discouraged in his favorite plan of organizing a Presbyterian Church. He was a Presbyterian in principle, and could not be Arminian through policy; however others might act, and besides he had commenced a great work among the people, sustained and upheld in it by godly and disinterested men, and having, as he believed, the sanction of the Most High. He would not, he could not come down from his work and stoop to such paltry littleness as was proposed. From that time to the day of his death I am informed no man dare approach him with any such miserable offer. In this attempt we conceive that there were some in the community who were regarding this Presbyterian effort with a jealous if not an evil eye. No doubt they saw the impressions made through the labors of Mr. Gloucester, and hence the attempt to crush in the very bud the entire thing. Some, no doubt, were like the Ephesians at the preaching of Paul, conceiving, if he was not checked, their gains would be gone, and would, did they dare do it, stir up the whole city against him, seeing their " craft was in danger to be set at naught, &c."

In a brief period of time about twenty-two persons were obtained from among the number that statedly attended upon the ministry of Mr. Gloucester; these were nine women and thirteen men, all hopefully converted to God, and with these he commenced his church by organizing them as a Presbyterian body. This was done, as near as we can arrive at the facts, about the latter part of May or early part of June in 1807. Mr.

Gloucester did not labor very long before there was a still further increase to membership.

During the first three years of Mr. Gloucester's labors in Philadelphia, he had very frequently to be absent in order to prepare himself for examination and ordination, as will be seen in a subsequent part of this narrative. During his absence, however, the wants of his little flock were attended to by his abiding friends, Drs. Alexander, Green, Janeway and Potts, one or the other of these gentlemen would watch over them and find time from their arduous labors to attend at least once a day on each Sabbath to preach to the people. Sometimes they would have to do as did Mr. Gloucester, go first to one place and then to another to meet the people and dispense the word of life to them; for at this time there was no "foot of ground they could call their own, nor cottage in this wilderness." They were without a house of worship of their own, and consequently they worshipped God wherever they could conveniently do so. Sometimes it would be a large room in Gaskill Street, at other times in the school-house in Seventh Street, near where the church now stands; however, wherever the people pitched their meeting in the absence of Mr. Gloucester, these benevolent Ministers of Christ would be found, and God rewarded them for their self-sacrificing spirit.

Such was the rapid increase at this time, 1809, that it was soon found necessary to adopt some plan or measures whereby a piece of ground could be obtained, and a house erected thereon, where the people could congregate, and their increasing numbers accommodated; hence, only two years after Mr. Gloucester entered upon his labors in Philadelphia such was the success that followed his efforts; and, abundantly blessed by the Most High,

4

that it was found necessary to make a strong effort to secure a building. Consequently, on July 31, 1809, the congregation appointed a committee to wait upon the Evangelical Society, and confer upon some plan whereby a house of worship could be secured. This committee met the society, and made their business known. With a promptness truly Christian the society at once appointed a similar committee to meet the committee from the colored people on the subject. After due consideration was had upon the matter, the committee from the Evangelical Society made to that body so favorable a report that the society ordered the following address to be signed by the President and published, and which I now insert not only because it may be regarded as a relic of that early day of Presbyterianism in Philadelphia, but of the excellent and Christlike spirit that it contains.

At a meeting of "The Evangelical Society of Philadelphia," held July 31st, 1809, the committee appointed to confer with a committee from the people of color on the subject of erecting a house of worship for their use, made a report which was approved, and the following address ordered to be signed by the President and published.

TO THE PIOUS AND BENEVOLENT.

The attention of the pious and benevolent is now called to a consideration of the condition of the people of color, in this city, as it relates to the means of religious instruction. The population of this description of people has of late become very numerous amongst us, and is daily rapidly increasing. The education of most of them has been extremely defective; and many have come here with habits very little compatible with the peace and good order of civil society. Your officers of police, your guardians of the poor, your justices of the peace, your criminal courts, your prisons and work-houses, can all attest, how much need there is of a reformation among the blacks of this place. This degraded state of manners cannot justly be attributed to any national inferiority, but must be entirely ascribed to the circumstance of a great part of them having so lately emerged from a state of abject slavery calculated to paralyze every noble faculty of the mind, and extinguish every moral sentiment; but every day furnishes us with increasing evidence, that the African race is not inferior to the inhabitants of the other quarters of the world, either in the natural endowments of the understanding or the heart.

It cannot be denied that there are many exceptions to the general remarks which have been made, respecting the degraded state of the people of color in this place. It is well known and must afford pleasure to every benevolent person, that there are some of them, who, in respect to intellect and moral improvement, rank high among their fellow citizens: but these are among the first to acknowledge and deplore the wretched situation of a large porportion of the people of color. And it deserves to be mentioned to their praise, that they have lately instituted a society, the express object of which, is to ameliorate the condition of their brethren *according to the flesh*, by the suppression of vice and the communication of moral and religious instruction among them. And will not every friend of virtue and good order among the whites, lend his aid in promoting this good work? Are we not bound by every consideration, of justice, of charity, of humanity, and of self-interest, to give our best assistance towards civilizing and reforming this numerous and increasing class of inhabitants? And what means so effectual for this purpose as the faithful preaching of the Gospel? The restraints of civil law are acknowledged to be salutary and necessary, and the influence of public opinion on the conduct of men is not to be despised; but after exhausting all our ingenuity in planning schemes of reformation, *the preaching of the Gospel* will maintain its importance, as the most successful and only effectual means of producing radical reformation among men. But in speaking of the good effects of the Christian religion, it would be unpardonable to confine our views to the present world. Its chief praise, is, that it is "able to make men wise unto salvation." Shall we, then, who profess a religion whose very essence is benevolence, be indifferent to the eternal salvation of our fellow men? Shall we suffer them to perish through "lack of knowledge," when it is so much in our power to supply them with the means of instruction? And that too when we have been accessary, as a people, in bringing them into their present wretched situation. The injury which has been done to this race of people by tearing them away from their friends and native country, and subjecting them and their posterity to a heavy yoke of bondage, cannot now be fully repaired; but that which was originally a crime of the most crying injustice and oppression, may, under the direction of a gracious Providence, prove eventually to be a blessing of the first magnitude, by bringing them in reach of the Gospel of Christ. But let us as far as it can be done, by acts of benevolence and charity to these people, wipe away the stain of our injustice; or at least obliterate the remembrance of it.

There are already, it is true, several African churches occupied by different denominations; but these are by no means sufficient for the accommodation of the thousands of people of color who now inhabit this city. It is believed, after some examination of the subject, that more than one-half of them are in no connection with any religious society, and seldom attend any place of public worship.

Besides, there are many, who, from education or principle, are attached to the Presbyterian Church. These find it to be inconvenient and unpleasant, for reasons which need not now be stated, to attend the houses of worship frequented by the white people. They are anxious to form a Presbyterian congregation among themselves, and they ought to be assisted and encouraged (*particularly by those who are connected with that denomination*), to carry their wishes into effect. And now a most favorable opportunity for accomplishing this object has occurred, which if suffered to pass without improvement, may not soon return. There is at this time in Philadelphia, a man of color, who is a licensed preacher of the Presbyterian Church, and has been employed by the committee of missions, to labor for some time among the blacks of this place. This man appears to be eminently qualified for extensive usefulness among the people of his own color. He has already attracted their attention and affections in a high degree. And if a place of worship sufficiently large, and conveniently situated, could be obtained, there can be very little doubt but what, in a short time, he would be able, by the divine blessing, to collect and organize a large society.

This object is so important, and the opportunity of carrying it into effect so favorable, that it is deemed unnecessary to add anything more by way of recommendation. There are many, it is believed, who need no stimulus to excite them to step forward with their aid: and it is confidently expected, that very few to whom application shall be made, will refuse their contribution; and although it be but a *mite*, yet it will not be overlooked by Him who appreciates a gift not so much by the amount bestowed, as by the willingness of the giver.

It is contemplated, as soon as sufficient funds can be collected, to purchase a convenient lot in the southwest part of Philadelphia, and to erect on it a house of worship, either slight and temporary, or substantial and permanent, accordingly as circumstances may dictate.

The public are therefore informed that within a few days, some persons duly authorized by the people of color, and others interested in their behalf, will begin to solicit the aid of the pious and benevolent to carry the object above stated into effect.

Resolved, That the money to be subscribed for the foregoing purpose shall be made payable to Messrs. ROBERT RALSTON, JOHN M'MULLIN, and FRANCIS MARKOE, who will stand pledged to the contributors for the faithful application of the funds to their destined object.

ARCHIBALD ALEXANDER,
President.

The subscribers, Pastors of Presbyterian churches in the city of Philadelphia, cheerfully and cordially concur with the president and their fellow members of the Evangelical Society, in earnestly recommending to the pious and liberal, the patronage of the design set forth in the preceding address, of erecting another church in this city for the accommodation and spiritual advantage of the people of color.

ASHBEL GREEN,
JACOB J. JANEWAY,
JAMES P. WILSON,
GEORGE C. POTTS.

In view of the circular being published, permit me to remark that this congregation was not a wealthy one, there were but few persons in it who were able to contribute any very considerable amount of money. The larger part by far could do but little in a monetary point of view; they wanted a house of worship, and they felt the necessity of it; they were willing, it is true, to do what they could, but willingness, however commendable, is not ability. All were ardent to have a piece of ground and the building erected; but ardency, though not condemnable, is not money; and however anxious the people might have been in their disposition towards the object, there was still wanting the available means to put the machinery in motion, the dollars were needful. This to them was the motive power only through which the work could be carried on or even commenced —here was the dilemma. Whilst they were at their wits' end, and everything looked lowering and dark, when no ray of encouragement illumined their hearts, the faithful pastor's voice was heard in accents of encouragement, exhorting them to rely on God and be of good cheer, for God who had been with them thus far would be with them to the end. It was at this time that he recommended a committee from the church to wait upon the Evangelical Society, as we have seen.

The publication of this circular proved so successful as to warrant the society and congregation at once to proceed in the matter. The lot at the corner of Shippen and Seventh Streets, where Mr. Gloucester so often stood and preached on Sabbath mornings, was secured. In less than one year from the publication of the circular, the corner stone was laid by Rev. George Potts, for a substantial brick church in 1810, and on May 31, 1811, it was dedicated to the service of God. This speedy progress was surely the Lord's doing, and it is marvellous in our sight, taking everything into the account. I must leave the reader to draw his own conclusions from this entire enterprise from its origin to the completion of the house in its rise and progress, if every step taken, and feature of it be considered. It will be remembered that in 1806 the matter was first agitated before the Evangelical Society. In 1807 the work of organizing the people into a Presbyterian

Church or body was commenced under the missionary labors of Mr. Gloucester. In 1810 the corner stone was laid, and in 1811 the church was dedicated to the service of God. All this was accomplished in four years, through the assistance of kind friends and the blessings of God.

Before passing on to a further notice of the history of the church, permit me to call the attention of the reader to one or two interesting things connected with the dedication of the church. It would seem upon so interesting an occasion, that Dr. Alexander should lead in the exercises of the day. He had previously removed to Princeton, and was one of the Professors at the Seminary. The people, encouraged and strengthened no doubt by Mr. Gloucester, made so unanimous and earnest an appeal to Dr. Alexander, that he consented to be present and preach the dedicatory sermon, assisted in the other exercises by Drs. Green and Potts. I am unfortunate in not being able to give the passage of Scripture on which the discourse was founded. I am equally so in not being able to give even a faint outline of the discourse, there being no record of the church upon which I can lay my hands to obtain the information. Of one thing we may be assured, it was appropriate and to the point.

Previous to the day of dedicating the house, Mr. Gloucester had the following address circulated among the people, and a copy sent to all friendly to his cause. For the address I am under obligation to Mr. Jacob C. White, Sen., who, very fortunately for the church and posterity, kept this relic in his possession, and which is now through his kindness given to all who may read these pages. It is the production of Mr. Gloucester's own brain.

I make no comment, but leave the reader to make his own inference of the man and his mind.

ADDRESS OF JOHN GLOUCESTER IN 1811, TO THE FIRST AFRICAN CHURCH.

Glad tidings of great joy to the African Race, and particularly to the infant Church, in which the hand of God has been so visible in collecting so many of us from the dark mountains of ignorance, sin and woe, to the bosom of the visible Church. The ground of our joy being somewhat similar to that ancient branch of God's Church who had been so long enslaved under the Babylonish yoke, but having accomplished the years of their suffering bondage, they were permitted to return to the land of Canaan and rebuild their temple. After they had begun this building they met with great discouragement which stopped the work of the Lord's house for eight years, after which time Ezra and the friends of Zion began and finished the temple, which was a subject of great joy to them and to all the well wishers of Zion, but terminated in the grief and confusion of their opposers. In like manner many of us have accomplished the years of our captivity, and returned to the land of blessed light and liberty. In the year 1810, a building was begun for the poor and afflicted sons and daughters of Ham, in Moyamensing district at the corner of Seventh and Shippen Sts., which was patronized by many of the worthy inhabitants of this city; we had the honor at the commencement of the building to have the following gentlemen go before us as the chief agents and planners of the work: Messrs. Ralston, F. Markoe, Captain Moore and John McMullin. By the pious exertions and influence of these gentlemen, united with many of the well disposed and benevolent inhabitants of this place, this house of worship was raised and made comfortable for use in the same year in which it was begun, but left in an unfinished state for two reasons: first, many of those who were free from temporal bondage were still willing to be slaves to sin and Satan, the worst of masters, however faithfully served, and the wages eternal death. Secondly, The number of those that seemed to be sensible of the invaluable blessings of the Gospel, and that of Christian liberty, were but few that attached themselves to this place of worship, and for them there was sufficient room, but since that time the Lord has increased us in number, and I hope somewhat in heavenly wisdom, so that many of those in years past who have undervalued the blessings of Gospel privileges have now learned how to appreciate them. As more room was wanting to accommodate those, which could be had by putting up the galleries in the church, this we took as a call from God to finish His house, which we attempted, some of us I hope like the builders in Ezra's day not by might or power, but by the spirit of God, hoping he will raise up for us unexpected friends to aid in carrying up the last stone of the temporal building as he did for them, for King Darius was made a nursing father to the church in his day, being overrated by the superintendent providence of God. He had the house of the rolls searched (wherein the treasure was laid up in Babylon), and there he found the decree of Cyrus, which he made in the first year of his reign, respecting the building of the house of the Lord, that it should be paid out of the King's treasury; this decree was enforced by King Darius, and the house was finished accordingly. In doing this, he fulfilled the prophecy and vision of Daniel respecting the Jewish Church. (Dan. Ch. 9th.) Now let the friends of Jesus look into the records of his decrees and see what he has said respecting the accomplishment of the Gospel church, and they will see his promises fulfilling in this day particularly as it respects Ethiopia, for she is now stretching out her hands to God or heart, through the means of Grace which she is now enjoying, and many of her sable sons and daughters are hopefully gathered in the bosom of the visible church, and as we are among that number glory is due to God from us, and humble thanks to that public spirit of benevolence which we have witnessed in this place. Having finished our building, we have set apart next Friday the 31st inst. as a day of thanksgiving to God for the innumerable blessings conferred upon us. The mode of spending this day will be in our private families in the morning, and at 3 o'clock in the afternoon we shall repair to the new finished building to present our public thank-offering to God, at which time there will be a sermon preached by a Rev. D. D., of Princeton, whose name I am not at liberty to mention, after which there will be a collection taken up to assist in defraying the expenses of this building, and we hope that those who gave us birth as a visible church will help this poor branch of God's vineyard in putting up the cap stone of this building, which is too high for our circumstances. Believing there is enough in the King's treasury, we throw ourselves at the feet of those with whom he has intrusted it, in hopes of receiving aid to finish a house which will stand as an eternal monument to the glory of God, the honor of the Christian religion in this place, and finally, we trust, will prove a blessing to many souls.

J. G.

We cannot very easily conceive of the deep throbbings of the people's hearts, and the intense interest felt by them, as the day broke in from amidst the gloom of night, when the building or edifice was to be dedicated to God; the time of their anxieties, the object of their hope, the finale of their fears, and the consummation of their desires, on that day were all to be realized—what thanksgivings to God in their families—what praising and rejoicing. Writing from this distant period, we can almost feel with them as we contemplate them around their family altars in their heartfelt gratitude to God, from whom came this good gift, and who enabled them to succeed in their undertaking. Surely there must have been a sacred joy springing up in every heart in that vast assembly of people, as they sat within those walls on that interesting occasion. That was a memorable day, made memorable, too, because heaven's God smiled upon them, and gave them tokens of approbation that he approved their labor of love, and accepted their offerings of praise and thanksgiving.

It is true the building was not in any way remarkable for architectural taste; it was a plain brick, sixty feet long by thirty-three feet wide, without any ornament about it either inside or out, but in this respect the people did what they could, with this assurance to encourage them, "that God does not require what a man hath not, but what he hath;" the offering, then, to God, of a plain, simple constructed edifice, is valued according to the ability of the people, and the spirit in which it is given to Him—hence the offering, though it might by many be regarded as insignificant, yet to Him who is God over all and blessed forevermore, attaches an importance to it that may not be entertained for a more costly and magnificent superstructure.

As we have seen, this building was dedicated to the worship of God in the year of our Lord 1811. It has four rows of pews, numbering seventeen deep, with two aisles three feet wide each, and will seat on the lower floor, very comfortably, 370 persons. It also has a gallery on each side and one on the end; these can accommodate 280 persons without discommoding each other. The ceiling is very high, which gives the audience-room a light and airy appearance. After the Church was finished and dedicated, the elders, trustees, and people, petitioned Presbytery to be taken under their care and inspection, to be considered in full standing as a Presbyterian congregation—"Whereupon, the Presbytery of Philadelphia did, on the 16th day of October, 1811, and sitting in Norristown, Pa., Dr. Janeway Moderator, and Dr. Green Clerk, receive under their care, according to their request, the African Church."

I will take this occasion to remark, now that the Church was received by the Presbytery, that Mr. Gloucester's relation with the Committee on Missions during his life, was never broken by his receiving a call from the congregation of the African Church, and consequently was never installed over them as its pastor, although he was all to them that a pastor could be, and was regarded by the people as a pastor beloved until the day of his death, and lives in the memory now of those who were children and youth at that time, with considerable veneration. His not being installed over the Church perhaps arose from the inability of the infant Church to provide for him as they could possibly desire, and to insure him such support as they desired to bestow if they could; hence to leave him in the hands of the Committee on Missions, and to assist the Committee as far as they were able of their ability, appears to be the reason why the call was not formally made out and put into his hands by his Presbytery.

The Church being now received under the care of the Philadelphia Presbytery, may be considered as forming one of the Presbyterian family, and as such, claims to be regarded in that light. Holding in common with all Presbyterian Churches their distinctive doctrines, which they are devotedly attached to from a conscientious belief of their Scriptural validity, as well also as Christ as its head, God blessed forevermore, and all his ministers as one in Him, and among whom none may claim any superiority over another, for all are brethren, Jesus himself the elder brother—the chief and only Bishop of the Church universal.

From the most reliable information that we are in possession of, the Church, at the time it was dedicated and received under care of Presbytery, comprised a membership of 123 persons. Mr. Gloucester has, in his address, assigned the reason why it was that the congregation, in its communion members, were so few; but there may be another reason, and that one is common to all Presbyterian Churches: as a general thing, they grow slowly, for the evident reason that the claims of the Gospel as preached by Presbyterian clergymen, are addressed more to the conviction of the conscience and understanding of the people, than to the prejudices and passions; hence, it may be presumed, that they are not very successful pioneers in a new enterprise: they are, however, good cultivators, and though their growth may be slow, yet they are sure and steady, striking root deep down in the virgin soil, that no rude blast nor passing storm can uproot nor tear from the regenerated sinner's heart, the doctrines of grace once implanted therein by power divine. Thus we account for the seeming tardiness of a great increase in a short space of time. As it is in nature so in grace: it is not the torrent of rain, as it comes pouring from the clouds, deluging the earth with its rushing waters, that invigorates, revives, strengthens, and vivifies vegetation, but rather the gentle shower or the soft falling dew that accomplishes this end, and to these agents in nature we more hopefully look for blooming fields, in their freshness and beauty so cheering to the eye and grateful to the heart. We are more than ever confirmed in this view of the subject, when we contemplate the ability, the zeal, the deep piety of the men engaged in preaching the Gospel to this people—their names alone convey the idea that each one was a host in himself—eminent for learning, remarkable for piety, and "not slothful" in Christian labors, is an attestation of the fact that the work, though slow at first, was still gradual and sure in its progress, as we shall see hereafter.

I must here remind the reader of what I asserted in the commencement of this history, that this African Church was the first and only Presbyterian one in Philadelphia, and in the United States. There were other African Churches, as I have stated, but not of this denomination. Being a new enterprise or effort in the face of older and established organizations, our wonder if any should cease, when I say that the people took considerable time to weigh well its claims before they gave in their adhesion to it: they could not be blamed for this caution, when we reflect that it is wise and commendable to weigh well in every point of view every proposition made as a matter of faith and practice, and in the light of reason and revelation pass judgment upon it before we decide to make it the object of our faith—the rule of our life. When this is done, then, like Dr. Young's good man, we may say with him, "Here is firm footing—solid ground," and so far as our belief and reception of the truth is concerned, may also add with him, "All else is sea beside; his hand the good man fastens on the sky, then bid earth roll nor feel its idle whirl."

We now regard the Church as fairly under way, launched forth upon the ocean of life, freighted with immortal souls bound for the shores of immortality and heavenly bliss. Oh, what a thought is this, an infant Church, to go out on the ocean of life to contend with the furious storms incidental to life, and the management of it intrusted to mortal hands. Well might the minister exclaim with Paul, "Who is sufficient for these things?" With John Gloucester and his faithful few, in view of all their difficulties, from this time there was one determination, and that was, to "work while it was day," to work amid every opposing force, each one adopting the Christian's decision:—

"In every trouble sharp and strong,
My soul to Jesus flies;
My anchor hold is firm in Him
When swelling billows rise."

The first two elders elected by the people to assist Mr. Gloucester in the spiritual wants of the Church, were Messrs. James Prosser and Cato Freeman. These continued to labor until the growing wants of the Church called for more laborers in this particular department of the Lord's vineyard, when Mr. Quamany Clarkson, a member of Dr. Janeway's Church, a man of piety, was importuned, and finally consented to join the African Church, and give himself to the work as an Elder therein: he was accordingly set apart for the office by Mr. Gloucester, through the call of the people. For years afterward we find Mr. Clarkson punctually representing his Church at the Presbytery, and seldom absent. His promptness in every duty was said by his contemporaries to be proverbial—truly, he was a shining light in Zion. The next Elder elected by the people, was Jacob Craig, mentioned in the early part of this work: he, too, was a faithful servant to his God and to his calling. These brethren continued to officiate in the Church during the whole period of Mr. Gloucester's life and ministry, and like him, labored earnestly to advance the glory of their Lord, and the best interest of his Church.

Of the time and circumstances of Messrs. Prosser and Freeman's election and setting apart for the office and duties of elders, we have no record. Unfortunately, a circumstance arose in the Church, which will be stated hereafter, that deprived the remaining session of the book of proceedings, and which, if their election and setting apart be therein recorded, I know not; the books until this day, not being in the possession of the present session. This is lamentable, for much useful information might have been gleaned from it, and the brief history I am now necessarily compelled to record, for the want of dates, &c., to say the least, might have been made more satisfactory.

It is gratifying, however, to look back upon the early labors of these Christian fathers, and behold their labor of love, and how they wrought in their Master's service. May it not be truthfully said of them, "Well done, good and faithful servants?"

Before passing on to other matters connected with this Church, I must call attention to the interest taken in the Church by the Presbytery of Philadelphia, at the time when the property was being purchased. The Evangelical Society addressed a communication to Presbytery upon the subject, to which they responded favorably by the following resolution, dated April, 1810:—

"*Resolved*, That all the Churches within our bounds be recommended, so soon as convenient, to take up collections for the said purpose, and transmit the same to Mr. Isaac Snowden."

These collections were made, and through these sources, together with those already alluded to, the people and their friends were able, as has been seen, to collect at least the largest part of the money required in order to a commencement.

In reviewing the past, it is a pleasing reflection, and reminds the people of this Church of the good King Hiram of Tyre, who, when Solomon would build the Temple of the Most High, "rejoiced greatly, and sent to Solomon saying, I have considered the things which thou sentest to me for, and I will do all thy desire, concerning timber of cedar, and concerning timber of fir. My servants shall bring them down from Lebanon unto the sea, and I will convey them by floats unto the place that thou shalt appoint me, and will cause them to be discharged there, and thou shalt receive them, &c., and Solomon's builders, and Hiram's builders did hew them, so they prepared timber to build the house." The Presbytery has ever taken a deep interest in this Church, and ever been watchful of its interests. As a proof of this, I will direct attention to a fact. Before the building was completed, Mr. Gloucester was on his mission to raise money to purchase his wife and four children: during his absence the Presbytery became a nursing father to the Church. In their supplies for other Churches within their bounds, they were not unmindful of this Zion. Messrs. Neill, Ely, Paterson, Skinner, Engles, Chandler, Steel, and Wilson, were appointed by Presbytery to supply the pulpit at regular stated times; in short, this has ever been done by Presbytery, and the pastors have ever come cheerfully when circumstances arose to make it necessary.

Having traced the church from 1807 to 1811, when it was taken under care of Presbytery, we may now consider it as fully established and occupying a position among the Presbyterian Churches of the United States. In reviewing the struggles of this church during these four years, we cannot but be struck favorably with the perseverance and industry of the people amidst every discouragement growing out of their pecuniary condition; and particularly would it be so where, on the other hand, we reflect that with the major part it was something new to be thrown upon their own efforts, their own reflections and ideas; and how well they sustained themselves under it may be seen from the short time through which they accomplished so much. It should be remembered that their pastor, upon whom they depended to a considerable extent, could not remain very long with them at a time to strengthen their hands and encourage their hearts; for it was during these four years that he travelled extensively in order to purchase his wife and children. Surely we must admire the spirit that impelled the people, and the mind that determined them in pushing on this enterprise. Then if we consider the opposition encountered at the commencement of it, as I have already alluded, we must conclude that their determination was not only a mark of their sincerity, but a proof that their religious principles were founded in their duty to God, and a conviction that what they had undertaken was well pleasing to Him, whose sustaining hand upheld and strengthened them to the end.

There are some things in close keeping with Christian enterprises upon which I have written but little, and before I close this part of our history I shall avail myself of the opportunity of directing the attention of the reader. I do this for two reasons: the first is because it is due to our fathers, as showing a feature of character in them which we, their children, should not only possess, but diligently cultivate, and religiously impress upon our children. The second is to show the principle upon which they acted in every effort. These two reasons, when maturely considered, will be found to be more important and weighty than at first sight appears. Christian enterprises, unlike those of other characters, are not so much determined because necessary to be done, however essential and commendable this may be, but the views entertained of its importance, the principle that governs, and the motive that impels in their accomplishment, are the true elements to be regarded as the basis of action. This I conceive to be the true Christian view entertained, whether it relates to the giving an alm to the beggar in the street, or sending across the wide ocean, through missionary labors, the Gospel of the Son of God to the daily perishing heathen, or the raising of a congregation of religious worshippers, building a church edifice for the service of the Most High, or any enterprise whatever where Christian effort is required; unless the above element predominates, and enters into all of our actions, our efforts will, to every honest mind, be divested of its most intrinsic value. Our fathers acted upon the principle of religious or Christian duty to God, and the good of humanity, when they undertook to establish and build up this Zion; there was a conviction in their minds that what they were doing was for the advancement of God's glory among men to unborn generations, and conceiving it to be conducive to God's glory, they saw it was their duty to enter upon the work with all their heart, and soul, and strength. The question may arise to some, as it did to me, From whence those ideas? The answer is a ready one, and can be traced through every act during their life: it is "love to God." Upon this heaven-born principle were their motives based; hence their perseverance, industry, zeal, and success. Could they fail? Could they be discouraged? Upon this principle we determine the character of each man and woman associated with Mr. Gloucester. It is said by a writer that we are "imitative creatures;" in the matter under consideration, at least, I shall be willing to accept the assertion, and reiterate it, and say truly our fathers did imitate the blessed Jesus in this Christian effort. Jesus wrought his works from a principle: that principle was deep love for humanity; he had no selfishness in all he did, no other end in view but another's good, and not his own. Love was the principle that impelled him. In this our fathers were "imitative creatures;" hence their piety, Christian fortitude, and glorious success, and, as I firmly believe, their felicity and joy in the Kingdom of Glory. Another thought upon this subject before I pass on. It is not perceived in all or any of the measures proposed during the time of raising means for the building of this church, that any one thing was done not in perfect keeping with Christian principle, or one that would in the least invalidate or compromise any of its divine teachings. Our fathers were too well instructed in the nature and requirements of their holy religion to be led away by any extraneous appendages that may be hitched on to Christian profession; if anything was to be accomplished, they obeyed the Christian rule, and gave of their substance, as God had blessed them; they contributed themselves as they were able, and when they failed, after every effort on their part was expended, they then felt, as all Christians should feel, that they had claims on the universal Church of Christ for help; and wherever among God's people access can be had, there they had a right to make their wants known, and their case felt; conventional rules, regulations, and laws to the contrary, notwithstanding—these should be pushed aside when charity is needed, and Christian embarrassments made known. Theatrical shows, feasts, and entertainments (now extensively practised in the form of suppers and dinners), and all this train of paraphernalia, should be most religiously avoided, as tending to divert from Christian principle to the gratification of sensual pleasure. what else is it but taking the very livery of the wicked one to serve the God of glory with? This is not Christlike, neither, indeed, can be: to be Christian, all our efforts must spring from Christian principles.

SEPARATION OF THE CONGREGATION INTO TWO DISTINCT BODIES, AND ITS CAUSE.

It is not a pleasant task for me to record the misunderstanding that took place in the Church, whereby it was divided into two separate bodies; it was, and is still to be regarded as deplorable, but as a matter of history connected with the first African Church, it has to be put on record. In doing so, however, it shall be my conclusion to give the simple truth without partiality, and, I will take the occasion to remark, that whatever views I may express herein upon divisions and dissensions in churches or religious bodies, will be understood as having a general allusion, and will, I hope, be so entertained by the reader.

The congregation, as we have seen, was supplied by Presbytery with preaching from the death of Mr. Gloucester, and now feeling desirous of calling a minister to take the pastoral oversight of the Church, concluded to do so. Consequently, on the 1st May, 1823, the session met at the house of Mr. Francis Webb—present, Elders Jacob Craig, James Prosser, Peter McNeal, Quamany Clarkson, and Francis Webb.

Rev. Wm. Neill having been invited to moderate, the session proceeded to business by taking into view the wants of the congregation for a pastor. It was decided that as the growing wants of the Church demanded a settled pastor, therefore:—

Resolved, That the congregation be notified on the next Lord's day, from the pulpit, to convene on the Thursday following, at 4 o'clock P. M., in the church, for the purpose of electing a pastor, if such be their wish.

It was agreed by session, that the names of all persons entitled to a vote in the election be enrolled in a book, and each name called out as recorded, in order, and each person at liberty to vote as they may think most proper. And further, the session, to prevent all complaints and misunderstandings, recommend the trustees to notify all pew holders who are indebted to the Church, and desire to vote on this election, to meet the Pew Committee on Tuesday next, in the church, in the morning from 9 to 1 o'clock, and in the afternoon from 3 to 6 o'clock, for the settlement of any claims against them by the corporation, whereby they might be prevented from voting. It was also determined, that all persons producing receipts in full up to January 1, 1823, will be entitled to a vote in the election. (*Min. book, pages* 2–3.)

On Thursday, May 8, 1822, agreeably to public notice, the congregation met in the church, Dr. Janeway presiding. He opened the meeting by addressing the throne of Grace for direction in the business that called them together; after which, he gave a suitable discourse to the occasion, and informed the congregation that if it was their wish he would proceed to take the votes for the election of a pastor. A motion was here made for an indefinite postponement of the election. This motion was put, and lost, 53 voting for, and 79 against it.

The Moderator requested a nomination, when the Rev. Samuel E. Cornish was nominated. The Moderator asked if there was any other nomination. There being no other candidate offered, the congregation proceeded to ballot, which being done, the votes were counted, when it was found that 78 votes were in favor of Mr. Cornish, and 48 against him. Mr. Cornish was then declared elected. A call for Mr. Cornish was ordered, and the congregation directed the trustees and elders to sign the call when made out. The following named brethren were appointed as commissioners to prosecute it before Presbytery: Robert Douglas, Ezekiel Harmon, and Quamany Clarkson. (*Extract from Min., pages* 3 & 4.)

To say that this election passed off peaceably, would be more than I can venture to affirm. It would be a pleasant duty so to record it, but unfortunately for the church and the cause of the Redeemer, it created an unhappy state of things in the church. The minority (and it was by no means a small one) was opposed to Mr. Cornish, not on account of anything against his character as a man or a Christian; not because he was incapable of taking the pastoral charge of the church; not because his intellectual acquirements were insufficient; none of these considerations influenced them in voting against him, and, I am truly happy here to insert, for the information of the reader, and in justice to Mr. Cornish, that some who voted with the minority said to me personally, that nothing existed with them against him, either morally, socially, or religiously; that they respected him as a Christian and a gentleman; and their only reason for voting as they did, was, they preferred Mr. Jeremiah Gloucester, he being a son of their beloved and deceased pastor. However, to resume our narrative, the call was presented to Presbytery on the 15th October, 1822, sitting at Doylestown. Presbytery finding a warm opposition by a large minority:—

Resolved, That a committee of three ministers and two elders be appointed to visit the church, and inquire into the state of the congregation, and observe a season of fasting and prayer with them, and report at next meeting of Presbytery.

Revs. Boyd, Paterson, and Biggs, and Elders Messrs. Stewart and McMullin, were appointed. This committee attended to the instructions received from Presbytery, with what success the subsequent action of Presbytery will explain, for at a session held by the Presbytery, in the Second Church, on Nov. 28, 1822, the above committee made a report, that leave be granted to prosecute the call for Mr. Cornish before the Presbytery of New York, of which he was a member. This was acceded to by Presbytery, but during the session a minority report was received, and as it appeared to the Presbytery that there was not sufficient unanimity in the call of Mr. Cornish to render his ministry useful among the people, a committee was appointed to advise with and try to heal any division that may exist in the church. Dr. Wm. Neill, Messrs. McMullin and Bradford, were appointed.

This committee likewise attended to the business assigned them, for on July 1st, 1823, presbytery being in session, and the subject coming up for their action, it was considered, and finally resolved that leave be granted to the congregation to prosecute the call for Mr. Cornish; but the whole thing was for the present frustrated by the minority, they appealing to synod against the action of presbytery. To be brief upon this subject, for it is in no way pleasant to dwell upon, the entire matter was taken to synod upon the appeal, and the synod confirmed the action of the presbytery; consequently the commissioners were at liberty to prosecute the call. The decision of synod being made known to the minority, they appealed from the decision to the general assembly. Before the general assembly met, the minority concluded to drop the matter, at least so far as any action of the assembly may concern it.

In the mean time, however, both parties were not idle in their endeavors to obtain their several ends: this was unfortunate. If anything could have been done, at this juncture, to heal the unhappy differences between these brethren, how desirable and blessed would it have been! what a tremendous blow to the cause of Christianity, the progress of our own denominational interests in Philadelphia, the union and harmony among our people, would have been arrested. But alas the friends of the church were doomed to sad disappointment: that blow fell; it fell with fearful violence, and its effects are felt even at this late period, from which I am writing. How true it is that great effects from very small causes grow. So in this instance it was but a very little matter in the beginning, but it kindled a great fire among the people, which no earthly interference could extinguish, as we have, and will still further see. I have said why the minority opposed the call of Mr. Cornish to the church; I will here give their reasons for so doing more fully, and also their subsequent action.

It will be remembered that previous to the death of Mr. Gloucester he had written a letter to presbytery, recommending his son Jeremiah as a candidate for the Gospel ministry, and to be taken under care of presbytery. This young man was received under care of presbytery, and prosecuted his studies with energy, and his future was regarded by his presbytery and the church as encouraging and hopeful; the affections of a portion of the church clustered around him, and they regarded him as the future pastor of the church, as soon as he had finished his studies, and was licensed by his presbytery. In view of this, when the proposition was made to call a pastor to the charge of the church, these brethren, who were favorable to Mr. Jeremiah Gloucester, dissented from calling any one to the church; entering the plea that the presbytery had heretofore supplied the church with the first and most efficient ministers in the presbytery, and had ever entertained toward the church the deepest and greatest concern in all their interests; and as it would not be very long before Mr. Gloucester would be through with his studies, they would prefer waiting. To this, however, the other party objected, pleading the wants of the church; its spiritual interests, they said, were waning; they wanted a pastor to go in among the people in their houses, as in the church, to attend in sickness, and to visit among the families, and so keep up an interest for the church. Here then was the difficulty. Could one or the other of these parties have yielded, how much bitterness would have been avoided! I must be permitted here to record, in justice to the brethren who were in favor of calling Mr. Cornish, that, upon their side, they had no objection to Mr. Gloucester; they regarded him with much concern, and, indeed, tenderness, for he was the son of their deceased pastor; how else could they regard him but with interest? But as he had not finished his studies, and the spiritual wants of the people called so loudly for the services of a pastor, they felt that all personal partialities should be waived, in consideration of the spiritual wants among the people. Upon these opposite views I make no remarks; let every reader weigh them, and decide for himself. Every effort being expended to reconcile these parties, and there being no probable prospect of healing the differences, the minority concluded, after mature deliberation, to withdraw and form another church or congregation. To this end, on the 9th of March, 1824, not quite two years after the death of Mr. Gloucester, a petition, signed by seventy-five persons, was presented to presbytery, requesting to be organized into a Second African Church. This petition was protested against by the session of the church, upon the ground that, as the petitioners were either communicants or pew-holders, their petition be not granted until they shall comply with their engagements to the church, and be regularly dismissed; whereupon presbytery passed the following resolution: "Having heard the parties fully, and maturely deliberated on all the circumstances of the case, that this presbytery are fully satisfied that the parties which have existed in the First African Church are of such a nature that further attempts to reconcile them are inexpedient, and that it will be for the peace of the church, and for the promotion of the Gospel, that a Second African

Church, of our denomination, be organized in this city." (*Min. Presb.*, p. 366.)

It would be uninteresting to state what followed upon the division of this church, and it is just at this place we must recall to the mind of the reader what I said in the commencement of this narrative, that not having the early records of the church during Mr. Gloucester's life, prevents me from inserting in this history, no doubt, much that is really necessary to be known, for when the minority withdrew from the church, singular as it may seem, they took the records of the church along with them, and hence, the church was thrown upon the necessity of recording, as far as they were able from memory, their early history; and it has caused the writer no small amount of labor to obtain what dates and facts are herein recorded.

In dropping this disagreeable part of the history of the First Church in its division, and offering our reflections upon it and all other instances like it, I repeat again, that I wish to be understood as having a general allusion.

As it is in civil communities, so in religious ones. According to the manner in which matters are at present constituted, divisions, contentions and strife, will, in a greater or less degree, prevail. This state of things need not necessarily exist, particularly in the Church of Christ. It has, indeed, been argued by some, that in order to purge the church from corruption and error, these elements of discord are necessary and beneficial; and I have been told repeatedly, that as thunder and lightning purge and purify the atmosphere, so these conflicting elements in the church produce like results. But I think the apostle finds an answer to such an assertion, and as I am treating upon a purely religious subject, it may be in order to lay down his laconic question and answer to this very matter under consideration. He asks, then, "From whence come wars and fightings among you? Come they not hence, even of your lusts that war in your members?" Here, then, could we be permitted to look behind the screen, at the propelling power put into motion by men and parties in the church, or at the machinery that operates with its spur wheels and running gear, we would soon see how far a necessity goes for purging and purifying the church of the Redeemer of its errors and corruptions. I do not deny that God does exercise a moral government in the church, but that government is one so ordered in wisdom as to preclude the possibility of an error in its administration or in its results; but it is not in confusions and strife, for God's government is like himself, of order, as he is of love; and when, therefore, there are seen contentions and strifes in the church, the God of this world, and not the God and Father of our Lord Jesus Christ, has gotten by some means among the people, and sown these tares therein. O! that "God's people were wise," that they would deny themselves of every temper that brings contentions and divisions. There can be no good reason shown why any body of Christians should be divided, unless for prudential and beneficial purposes, and those for the interests of all concerned, founded all in Christian love. As an Apostle expresses, "Let all things be done in charity."

The church is represented in Scripture as the family of God. All who are spiritual members of it are his dear children by adoption, as well as by redemption. It seems clear, then, that they constitute his family on earth, as the angels are of his family in bliss. Can there be shown, then, why the same affection and interest in each other of the family on earth, should not exist as it does in the family in heaven? It is regarded as a very unhappy state where divisions exist in families, and we view it as truly deplorable where there are alienations and separations, and every virtuous and order-loving man regards it in that light. Is the church, then, for which the Saviour poured out his life blood, to be considered less important, less interesting, and less in the eyes of the Redeemer's blood-bought family, than the relations existing among us in our domestic and social ties, however sacred and tender they should be? Well for the church, for the world, and for the glory of Christ's kingdom, could this exceeding and deeply interesting subject be more considered, and receive our undivided attention. When will God's people love like little children? When will they see eye to eye? When the Saviour was born in Bethlehem, the song of the angels as heard by the wise men, was, "Glory to God in the highest—peace on earth, good will to men." When Jesus had grown from a babe to a man, and finished the work he came to do as sung by the angels, and was about to return into the heavens from whence he came, he left this blessed sweet gift to his precious and dear followers, "Peace I leave with you, my peace I give unto you. Not as the world giveth give I unto you," and yet again he says, "A new commandment I give unto you, that ye love one another as I have loved you, that ye also love one another. By this shall all men know that ye are my disciples, if ye have love one to another." What, then, shall we say when disputings and divisions prevail among God's people? Wo to that man through whom they come; it were better for him that a millstone were hanged about his neck, and he cast into the sea. It is regarded as a horrid cruel thing to distract and divide our earthly friends and break up family ties, and thus causing separation and estrangement, if not bitterness and wrath among them. Will not, does not God so regard it as a crime where a like course is pursued toward His family in the church? Will he not visit in sore displeasure any who wilfully, presumptuously, and knowingly divide his people? It requires no stretch of human insight to see the certainty of it, and let me remark here, that though for a season or time they may prosper and bid fair, and all their doings may seem clear and bright as a "bright midsummer's day," yet will the displeasure of the Almighty overtake them, and by his own mysterious way by which he governs the universe, sit as with a clear heat on their works and measures, burning and scorching up and producing such drought upon it as to make it evident that the face of the Almighty is set against them. "Though it tarry, yet will it come," saith the Lord.

Happy for Mr. Gloucester that no division took place in his day. It would have crushed and broken his spirit, no doubt, and brought him to a premature grave. But the good God spared him the sight of seeing the church of his care—the object of his prayers—the hopes of his future comfort in his declining years—distracted and riven asunder by those who were the companions of his trials, and his partners in his early struggles for the church.

The church being now divided, the only alternative left to the remaining members was to cast about and adopt such measures as were best calculated to advance their interest; in this they were not without the best advisers; the same friends that always stood by them did not forsake them in this time of their troubles; the presbytery once more became a nursing father to them;

they continued the pulpit supply, and saw that the ordinances of the church were attended to. From the time that the church was divided, the troubled waters of contention abated, the storm of confusion was stilled, and peace and order again restored in this house of the Lord; so that, from March 9th, 1824, when the receding party left, to the subsequent call of Mr. Hughes, everything went on as prosperously as could be expected under the circumstances that surrounded them; of course it must be presumed that, from the withdrawing from the communion of the church of so large a body as the minority was composed, it weakened considerably the church, and their efforts to some extent affected. To their credit, however, be it said, they staggered not at the promises of God; they knew in whom they believed, and on whose arm they leaned for support; they took courage from the past, and became hopeful of the future.

Their first act, after the division, was to renew the call to Mr. Cornish: they accordingly addressed a letter to him, and received an answer "that, as the matter of a call had been so long delayed, and that, as many changes had taken place since the commencement of the business, and on viewing the whole train of circumstances together, he thought it to be most prudent for him to decline the acceptance of the call," &c. This was reported in session, April 9, 1824, one month after the division took place. On the 14th April, 1824, the congregation met, Dr. Janeway presiding. After prayer by the chairman, he stated the object of the meeting, and, if agreeable to them, would proceed to take the votes of the electors for a pastor; they declared it by an unanimous vote. They then nominated Mr. Benjamin Hughes. There being no other person nominated, the congregation proceeded to ballot, when an unanimous vote was given for Mr. Hughes. A call was subsequently made out, presented to Philadelphia Presbytery, of which Mr. Hughes was a licentiate, and accepted by him. The Presbytery appointed the 4th May, 1824, as the time for his ordination and installation, and appointed Dr. Green to preside, Rev. Mr. Chandler to preach the sermon, Rev. Mr. Biggs, to deliver the charge to the pastor and people. On the day above specified, the Presbytery met in the African Church, Dr. Green presiding, Dr. Ely, clerk, present, Revds. Drs. Janeway, Potts, Neill, Biggs, Ballentine, Engles, and Scott, Rev. Mr. Arbuckle, of the Presbytery of Niagara, Rev. Mr. McInnes, of the Second Presbytery of Philadelphia, being present, were invited, and took seats. Dr. Chandler preached the sermon from Jer. xxvi. 15: "For of a truth the Lord hath sent me unto you to speak all these words in your ears." Dr. Green propounded the constitutional questions, and offered the ordaining prayer, during which the Presbytery imposed their hands. Mr. Biggs, in accordance to appointment, gave the charge to the pastor and people. The right hand of fellowship was then given Mr. Hughes, and he took his seat as a member of Presbytery. The interesting ceremonies being over, and the church, in possession of a new minister, at once assumed a cheerful appearance, for, during the brief period of Mr. Hughes' administration, some who had strayed away from the communion of the church returned, and whilst it may be true that there were none added, yet there appeared a brighter prospect dawning for them. But again was this church doomed to disappointment. Mr. Hughes, after remaining about six months, informed Presbytery that the support received not being sufficient to sustain him, he was compelled to engage in some mercantile pursuit, in order to sustain himself. The Presbytery appointed a committee to confer with Mr. Hughes upon the subject, and offer their advice and views upon it; the result of the consultation may be gathered from the fact that, on October 31, 1824, Mr. Hughes convened the session, and notified them of his intention to withdraw from the pastoral office he held, and on November 18, 1824, he laid his request of withdrawing before the Presbytery, which, after both Mr. Hughes and the elders of the church were heard, the request was granted, and the church declared to be vacant. Thus again was the church thrown upon Presbytery for supplies, and it was cheerfully granted. We have now to pass over a space of three years, during which time many useful reflections may be gathered, and many interesting occurrences observed: it could not be supposed otherwise. Here was a congregation laboring under so many discouraging circumstances, still holding out, and looking forward for better days. And what makes it interesting to the observant mind is that, in a city like Philadelphia, where there were such prosperous churches; so many zealous and efficient ministers; such progress and prosperity; such extension and addition to membership; such zeal and energy put forth by the efforts of these several church members to add to their several denominations, we think must have acted with tremendous effect upon this Presbyterian body. The Second African Church also, at this time, was in the full enjoyment of prosperity, with Mr. Jeremiah Gloucester as its pastor, a large and flowing attendance on his ministry: all calculated to crush out whatever of life might have remained in the old church. And again, it becomes more discouraging when we reflect that the prospect of obtaining another minister was com-

6

pletely cut off, for at the time of which I am writing there were but three colored clergymen in all the United States in connection with the Presbyterian Church. How sad and gloomy, then, the prospects of this church, when compared with all the rest. Of the three Presbyterian ministers alluded to, Mr. Cornish was interestingly engaged in New York, in an enterprise that has, under God, established many Presbyterian Churches in that State. Mr. Hughes, as we have seen, not only left his pastoral charge and engaged in mercantile speculations, but left the city, in fact the United States, and when last heard from was in Africa, where, after a brief stay, he died. And Mr. Jeremiah Gloucester was then over the Second African Church. The Methodist churches, at this time, were in full blast. Rt. Rev. Richard Allen had recently drawn out from the Methodist Episcopal Church, and set up an independent organization, governed and controlled by black men, whither the people were flocking by thousands, as we shall see at the end of this volume. The fact that preachers in abundance were scouring the city with true missionary courage and zeal, and compelling people of all kinds, and of all characters, to come in, pressed also with no small effect upon this First Presbyterian Church.

St. Thomas' Church, also, with Rev. Absalom Jones as its pastor, the fast friend of Mr. John Gloucester, was in the glory of her strength, throwing a mighty influence in the city among the intelligent and refined. Casting a steady and intensifying heat in that direction, she drew to her communion and embrace the wealth and talent of Philadelphia; what chance then in this direction for the First African Presbyterian Church. And here I will say that St. Thomas' members (like their pastor) never forsook the old church; they were ever friendly, and are so until this day, and it is no uncommon sight at present, on the first Sabbath afternoon of every month, for many of them to be found worshipping in this Church; but, however, all things considered, it must be allowed that the prospects of the church were discouraging, to say the least of it; but, my readers, there were strong men in the old church; there were Boanerges there, men of God, valiant men, men whose hearts were full of love to God, and full of zeal for His glory in the church, and considered no labor too great, no sacrifice too dear, and no discouragement so gloomy, as to deter them from laboring on, and laboring ever, to build up their Zion; there was that stanch old man, Quamany Clarkson, the early and tried colaborer with Mr. Gloucester, and no less so Peter McNeal, in spirit like unto Peter; there, also, was Jacob Craig, another faithful elder of the church; and of the trustees, Messrs. Robert Douglass, Ezekiel Harmon, Abr. Depee, Wm. Hollis, with many others, all strong men, full of faith and energy—with them labor was no task, duty no load; therefore, they harnessed themselves for the battle, and went forth depending upon the Lord from Heaven for final success. They well understood that Scripture, "In the morning sow thy seed, and in the evening withhold not thy hand, for thou knowest not which shall prosper, either this or that;" they took courage from the promises of God, and worked on in hope. From the records in my possession there does not appear to have been many additions to the church by persons either through profession of faith or certificate, yet I find everything as peaceable and calm as under the peculiar circumstances of the case we could reasonably expect, if, during these three years, as above referred to, there was no increase of membership, at least, there was no falling off of members, and no waning of spirituality among them, and herein is a peculiarity in God's people evidenced under afflictions and distresses their faith and confidence become strongest; it appears to be the time when the people of the Most High are aroused up to a closer examination of themselves; it is then that every grace in the soul is fully drawn out, and from amid the clouds of distress and tribulations they look to God "as their only help in every time of need," and I do not venture too much when I say it appears to be an ordeal through which the Most High brings his people; at any rate, such is the view that His word holds out; if any doubt, they have but to turn to that highly interesting passage to be found in Revelations, chapter 7, 14th verse, where it is said to John, "These are they which came out of great tribulation, and have washed their robes, and made them white in the blood of the Lamb." Impressed no doubt with the truth of this assertion, consequently resting upon it as the Lord's way in dealing with his children, and following as near as possible the example of their blessed Saviour the Lord Jesus, these brethren, in the midst of every discouragement, rose superior to them all, and held together, awaiting the Master's own time for some favorable change in their peculiar and trying case, of three years' "patient continuance in well doing." About this time, 1827, the Rev. Charles Gardner, a minister of the Methodist denomination, in deacon orders, came into Philadelphia, and, being a man of a large heart and extensive liberality in his Christian principles, was solicited to preach for the congregation, and such was the effect upon the people, and their appreciation of his manner and mode of applying and enforcing the doctrines of grace, that in Oct., 1827, the congregation applied to Presbytery, then sitting at Bridgetown, for leave to employ Mr. Gardner as a stated supply until the spring meeting of Presbytery, whereupon Presbytery authorized Drs. Janeway and Ely as a committee to examine Mr. Gardner as to his qualifications to discharge the duties of his sacred office. This was attended to, and he was authorized to supply the pulpit until further notice. Mr. Gardner then entered upon the duty, and preached his first sermon in that capacity on Sabbath, Dec. 1st, 1827. Mr. Gardner continued to preach until the spring. At this Presbytery, the church made application for the services of Mr. Gardner until the next meeting of Presbytery, which was granted. On Nov. 10, 1829, Presbytery being in session, proceeded to examine Mr. Gardner with a view to his licensure; but before the examination was ended they referred his case to a committee, appointed when the Presbytery adjourned. On April 21, 1830, Presbytery being in session, the Committee to whom was referred the final examination of Mr. Gardner reported to Presbytery that Mr. Gardner requested to be dismissed from under their care, which report was accepted. Here was another terrible blow for the church, and one calculated to prostrate the energy and hope of the people, building their future prospects under God upon Mr. Gardner, believing that a beneficent Providence had so ordered it that he should visit and labor among them, and being also delighted with his preaching, for he was certainly no mean expounder of the Word of the Lord, all of these considerations were calculated to discourage and dishearten. Of course, there was no other alternative but Christian-like to yield submissively to this stroke and accept of it as being of the Lord, and whatever he did was right, marvellous as it might appear; of one thing they were certain, that was, inasmuch as there was no misunderstanding between Mr. Gardner and them, they considered that his motive was pure for making the request of Presbytery, and his reasons, not based upon any disposition to injure the church, from all we could understand, it was simply some points of doctrine to which, for the present, not fully understanding so that he could conscientiously subscribe to them, he required time for reflection and decision; this was worthy of him, and Presbytery so considered it.

MR. CLARKSON'S DEATH.

There are times in the history of a church, as there are in the life of individuals, when afflictions and discouragements enter into all their arrangements, prostrating their energies, and often filling the soul with anguish and despair. True, it sometimes happens that they are as dark clouds that flit across the Christian's sky, and hide for a time the brightness of his sun. This is so common in every relation of life, whether as men or as communities, that I need say no more upon it, for observation, if not experience, must concede its truthfulness. This was particularly the case with the church at this time. It was not quite three months from the time of Mr. Gardner's withdrawal from the church, when the death of Mr. Clarkson was announced. On July 2d, 1830, he closed his eyes in death, aged 65 years. It is true the people knew that from his failing health he could not long survive, but expecting, as they did, that he would shortly be called away from earth, yet they were not prepared to hear so soon that their elder, their venerated father in Israel, would be so suddenly called. Of Mr. Clarkson much might be said, but we have spoken of him in another place; let it suffice me here to remark, the life that Mr. Clarkson lived he lived by faith in the Son of God, so that when he fell asleep, it was in Jesus.

In September, 1830, Presbytery again granted supplies for the church, and during this period there was some increase. The number of communicants usually in attendance upon the communion, numbered about forty persons; a reduced number, certainly, to what was once the communicants of the church, when things wore a brighter aspect, that is, before the division took place. However, they did not disregard "the day of small things;" they thanked God for present blessings, small though they might be—took courage therefrom, and still looked to God and labored on. On July 10th, 1831, notice was given that the church was in need of another elder, to assist in the spiritual wants of the church. The old elders were fast failing, and being enfeebled through excessive labors, and younger men were now required. Accordingly, Mr. Thomas Black, a man of piety and strict integrity, with business qualifications such as the house of the Lord required, was the choice of the people as a candidate; whereupon, on July 31, 1831, Mr. Black was set apart, and ordained by the Rev. George Potts, as an elder of the church. About this time, also, the church made another application to Mr. Samuel Cornish, at New York, with a view of obtaining his service to supply them with the Gospel. To this appeal Mr. Cornish responded, and on December 13, 1831, Mr. Cornish commenced his labors among the people, which he continued to do with considerable success until the month of June, 1832, when, from circumstances of an interesting and important nature to him, and his calling to another field of labor, he resigned his care of the church.

On July 3, 1832, Dr. Green being appointed by Presbytery to moderate the session of the church, and administer the communion of the Lord's supper, &c., to the people, entered upon the duties.

On Feb. 22, 1833, Mr. John Burch being previously offered and accepted by a majority of the people, Dr. Green proceeded and ordained him a ruling elder to serve the church. From the time Dr. Green took the care of the church, as above stated, to the time of his resigning, on April 30, 1835, over two years, there was considerable increase, and much regret was expressed by the congregation on account of his withdrawal. I will here insert, without the least fear of any one soul in the congregation demurring against the assertion, that the church will ever cherish towards the memory of Dr. Green, the deepest regard and reverence—"though dead" yet to them "he liveth."

On July 29, 1835, Mr. Nathan Harned moderated the session and became the supply to the church, and continued faithfully in discharging the duties imposed upon him by Presbytery until May 6, 1836, at which time the congregation met and determined to elect a pastor, according to notice previously given. Whereupon, the Rev. Charles W. Gardner, having returned to Philadelphia and become a member of the Philadelphia Presbytery, was unanimously chosen, and the elders and trustees were authorized to fill up and prosecute a call before Presbytery. Mr. Thomas Black was appointed to present the call. The call was presented to Presbytery and put into the hands of Mr. Gardner, and accepted by him. July 5, 1836, was set apart as the day to install

Mr. Gardner. Dr. Green was appointed to preside; Rev. Mr. McCalla to preach the sermon; Dr. Green to put the requisite questions to the pastor elect and the people; and Mr. Blythe the charge to pastor and people.

The text chosen by Mr. McCalla was 2 Timothy, chap. i. 13 v.: "Hold fast the form of sound words which thou hast heard of me." I need not say much concerning this highly interesting occasion; it may suffice me merely to remark that the interest seen and felt on that occasion may be gathered from the dense mass of people that filled the house that day. It seemed as if the great Head of the Church opened upon them a day-spring from above; rays of light broke through the gloom of years, and the clouds of discouragement, that hung so heavily over them and casting their dark shadows across their pathway for the three years that they labored without hope of a settled pastor, were dispelled on that day, and light, bright, glorious light, came flooding in on that faithful band of men and women, who for years combated so nobly against such fearful odds as I have frequently described in this narrative. The installation and its stirring emotions of the day, will long be remembered by the church.

From this time, then, Mr. Gardener must be regarded as the settled pastor of the church. Under his ministry the addition of members was numerous, and the increase of the congregation very large: insomuch that the building could scarcely accommodate the number of persons that attended on his stated ministry. Of the elders officiating at his installation were Peter McNeal, Thos. Black, and John Burch. These brethren labored with Mr. Gardner during his pastoral charge, excepting to some extent in the case of Mr. McNeal, who departed this life on the 10th January, 1841, at the ripe age of 75 years, after serving his Lord and Master, as an elder in the church, for the space of thirty years. He was a man full of zeal for the glory of the Lord's house, and though bending under the weight of years, yet his ardor was not cooled, nor his interest in the church in the least abated. As he lived, so he died: with heaven in his view, the promises of his God to lean upon, and the grace of Christ to sustain, cheer, and lighten up his pathway as he "walked through the dark valley and shadow of death." The church mourned his loss sincerely, for they deeply felt "that a great man had fallen in Israel," when death laid its iron arm upon him, and laid him in the dust. He is gone, but what is loss to the church is gain to him. We believe, from the life he lived, the death he died, that he has entered into that rest that remains for the people of God. Such was the increase of members that joined the church, and the press of business upon the pastor and elders, that it was found necessary, about this time, to seek out a man upon whom some of the growing wants of the church might be apportioned. Such a man was found in the person of Mr. Jessie Turner, then a young man of deep piety, sound judgment, and possessed of a large share of discrimination, qualities necessary to constitute an efficient elder. Such being the views entertained of Mr. Turner, he was elected to the office of a ruling elder, and ordained by Mr. Charles Gardner, on the 19th day of January, 1840. At the time that Mr. Gardner became the pastor of the church, there were about 130 members. It will be borne in mind that the membership was reduced to the stated number on account of the division that took place, and some by removals to other locations, and a few by death, so that my readers need not be surprised at the meagre number presented. However this might be, Mr. Gardner did not labor very long before a happy and charming change for the better became evident. Many that had wandered away from the fold returned, and not a few from the gay world of fashion and pride earnestly sought the Lord, and found peace in believing on Jesus, and were received into the church. Many were the precious seasons of grace enjoyed by the church, under the ministry of Mr. Gardner. It was a soul stirring time, in these days—a time of refreshing from the Lord. The old and the young "came inquiring for him of whom Moses and the prophets did write." It was a common sight, on communion seasons, to behold a goodly number sitting around the table of the Lord, for the first time, who, a few weeks before, were indulging themselves in the frivolous and foolish enjoyments of the world, without a thought, scarcely, of those serious and important considerations of death, judgment, and eternity. Now "they were clothed in their right mind." Having professed faith in Christ, "they conferred not with flesh and blood, but took up their cross and followed the Saviour."

Such was the continued increase of the congregation and its growing wants, particularly in view of the large number of young persons connecting themselves with the church, and also the very encouraging prospects of the Sabbath-school attached to the congregation, that it was thought both prudent and necessary to obtain the service of another elder, possessing qualifications to engage in the evident wants of the church, among the young as well as the old. To this end, Mr. Jacob C. White seemed eminently qualified; his literary attainments, his Christian and consistent deportment, his remarkable zeal and piety, pointed to him as a man for the office of an elder, and the finger of providence manifestly singled him out, and so the people considered it; consequently the session met, after obtaining the consent of Mr. White, and he was examined, and, giving satisfaction of his qualifications, was accepted by the congregation, and ordained on the 18th October, 1842. There were now four elders constituting the session; these remain until this day, with the exception of Mr. Jesse Turner, who, having served the church faithfully, and beloved by the whole church, and by all who knew him, and above all we believe by his God, calmly, peacefully, and full of faith in God, leaning on his Redeemer, closed his eyes in death on the 25th of April, 1853.

Mr. Gardner remained pastor of the church for near twelve years, when he notified the congregation that, on the coming session of the Presbytery, he should ask a dissolution from the pastoral relation to the church, whereupon, on the 14th day of February, 1848, the application being made to Presbytery, and granted, the congregation consented to the dissolution, by passing the following resolutions:—

Resolved, That, although we entertain an affectionate regard for our pastor, yet as it is his desire to be released from the connection which has for several years so happily subsisted between him and us, we consent to his request.

Resolved, That it is our sincere prayer that the blessings of God may accompany him through life, and render him both useful and happy.

Thus terminated the ministry of Mr. Gardner over the church, a ministry, to a considerable extent, of usefulness and improvement. Many are now members of the church who are seals of his ministry, and some bright and shining lights are now members of it who have been brought from darkness to light, and who will ever regard Mr. Gardner with affection. In reviewing the labors of Mr. Gardner, we are strongly reminded of the interesting reviving times of Mr. Gloucester, for during the pastoral oversight of Mr. Gardner the congregation presented a cheering and highly gratifying appearance. The church was not only numerously attended, so that there was not room to contain the congregation, but the press of young people from the respectable and intellectual portion of the community, was encouraging. These finally became so deeply interested in his exposition of the doctrines of Christ, that scores of them gave their hearts to God and connected themselves with the church. I assume that no church of color in Philadelphia, and I omit not one, could compare with this church at this time (1843), for the number of young intellectual persons that were members of it. The frequent revivals that took place in 1842 were soul-cheering and reviving, showers of refreshing from on high came pouring down during the major part of this year. I will give a few of the number received into full communion on an occasion or two: Jan. 5, 1842, 8 received; Jan. 17, 14 received; Feb. 15, 12 received; Feb. 23, 20 received; April 3, 11 received; April 6, 3 received; May 11, 27 received; and so during nearly the whole of this year, it was the day of God's power to make willing the hearts of the young. Here in four months ninety-five young interesting persons were brought by the power of the Word of Christ. As a matter of course, we are not to suppose that during these twelve years there were no trials to endure by Mr. Gardner and the elders; to presume it, would argue but a very shallow insight into human affairs, and I am yet to learn from the present constitution of things by which we are surrounded, if there can be any situation in life clear of embarrassments, troubles and cares. The church is no exception, and though we should expect peace, prosperity, love, and harmony to prevail, considering the use, the aim, and the end of it, observation, if not experience, shows that to some extent, at least, these desirable ends are scarcely attained. As long as human nature remains clothed with mortality, so long will imperfections exist. We cannot close our eyes to the fact that evils exist in the human heart. They are latent for a time, snugly hid away, but ready to leap forth when an occasion offers. How often are we surprised at the sudden springs of these latent evils ourselves. They should be stormed and rooted out from the citadel by a Divine power; like rank weeds springing up in a garden, however well attended, they require to be pulled up and cast out by the careful husbandman. So must the pride, passion and lusts of the professor be carefully watched, and every root of bitterness cast out as soon as it appears. Like David, we should ever pray, "Search me, and try me, and see if there be any evil way in me."

It will form no part of my duty to venture any remarks upon the motive or reason why Mr. Gardner resigned the pastoral charge of the church. According to the resolutions passed, it can be discerned that the separation was a friendly one, and such should always be the case between a retiring pastor and the people. It often happens that chief friends are called to part, not in bitterness but in love. Many circumstances may arise to make it necessary, without altering in the least the interest and affection existing. Such, I believe, was the case in this instance. Mr. Gardner still lives, though well advanced in years, and very recently visited the city and preached to the people, by whom he was received most cordially. He still retains, apparently, the vigor of a strong man, and although in the 73d year of his age, his voice is still clear and strong. In intellect and energy there is no marked difference to what it was years long past.

But to proceed with this narrative, I must remark, that after the pulpit was declared vacant, the church was once more thrown under the fostering care of Presbytery, and they supplied the pulpit, as they had ever done when the wants of the church required it. The church remained without a pastor for about seven years, during which time Rev. Griffith Owen, Dr. Cuyler, and Dr. Joseph H. Jones, not only moderated the session, but took a deep interest in all the affairs of the church, administering the communion or the Lord's supper, baptizing the children, advising and counselling with the elders as to every measure whereby the church could be benefited. During this period of the church history, there was considerable exertion made to obtain the service of a pastor, so as to relieve the Presbytery and the gentlemen appointed by them to moderate the session, from so burdensome a service; at least, so thought the session, for I must inform the reader that each of these brethren had their own congregations to attend, and their congregations were very large, yet we cannot advance a single proof or any idea whatever, that they were not perfectly willing to do all in their power for the interest of this branch of Christ's church. It was during this time that various and frequent calls were made to pastors to take the pastoral charge, but without success. This, no doubt, arose from the fact that there are few Presbyterian colored ministers, and these were all settled over their several congregations or churches, and it must be perceived that the inducements to break these relations must be sufficiently strong; and so it appeared in the cases upon which we are now treating. The finger of God must clearly point the course a pastor should pursue in such a case. To leave a charge on slight grounds, or simply that a call is made for services desired by another congregation, forms no part of a pastor's consideration. There may be instances where it may be duty to break these relations, as when a people, from some cause, or source, or rumor, loses confidence in a pastor, or when from some motive or circumstance he is no longer useful among them, or even when his ministry is not blest or of spiritual interest, it may be his Christian duty and obligation to resign his charge, that an opportunity may be afforded some other to take the pastoral oversight, whose labors may be more successful. But in all such cases, I repeat, God's direction must be sought, and not a step taken until it shall appear clear as a sunbeam that such are the leadings of Providence. Such, perhaps, may be the reasons we can best produce why these calls were not accepted, and why the church remained so long without a pastor.

It is not to be presumed, in a city like Philadelphia, a city of churches, and where there are so many enterprises, influences, and engagements of every color and description, that a church without a regularly installed minister, can hope to retain its membership. We need not be surprised at this statement, when we reflect that we are in an age of the world when proselyting from one denomination to another has become the fashion of the day, and particularly among some sectarians. Wherever this is seen and done, it is censurable and condemnable, if not abject, to say the least of it. On the other hand, in many instances, the glitter and gayety of life, with its thousand attractions, prove too strong a current for many to resist. Especially is this so with the young, whose principles of Christianity have not been firmly fixed on Christ, as the rock from which they see things. There are other considerations that may be offered why a congregation may be reduced where there is no settled pastor. These that I have stated may be sufficient for the present, leaving the reader to reflect upon many others that may be adduced for this dwindling away of the church of which I am now writing, as well as if I had been careful to mention more, or describe instances in particular. However sadly the church was reduced in numbers, there was one singular feature always existing in it—there were those of its members who were so devotedly attached to their Zion, that no possible discouragement could shake their love for it. Minister or no minister, their affection for their church was deep and abiding, and though at times it appeared that to obtain a pastor seemed as hopeless and disheartening as can well be conceived, yet this small band of men and women remained like faithful soldiers at their post, and when through every effort of designing individuals, offers and inducements were held out, and every subterfuge resorted to in order to break up and destroy this branch of the church, there were those in it who, like the disciples of old, were determined, though all forsook this mother church, that they would not forsake her; and they did not, as the sequel of this history will show. It is to be regretted that there was such a waning of membership during this period, still the Master was not unmindful of his church. Now and then an application would be made by some to become members, and thus at times the Lord would

7

revive the spirits of his people, and give them a refreshing shower from on high.

In the year 1854 the congregation, in view of the antiquated appearance of the church, and the necessity of remodelling it, concluded to enter into some measures for accomplishing so desirable an end. It may not be known to the general reader of these pages why it was that at this particular, and to human probability, discouraging period that the congregation should attempt the remodelling of the building. Philadelphia, it is well known, by all who are acquainted with the fact, contains a colored population of intelligence and wealth as can be found in any city in the Union, and possessed of considerable taste.

The colored churches of this city are confirmatory of this fact; in their interior as on the exterior they present an appearance of neatness and good taste. Those that have recently been erected have been built in keeping with the latest architectural style of whatever order. As a general thing, all old churches have been remodelled and made to present a respectable appearance. I do not by any means wish to convey the idea that they have been extravagantly remodelled; simplicity and neatness alone have been substituted for the dull and sombre appearance of the old buildings. To these churches thus remodelled people preferred to worship, particularly that portion of the community which should by some means or other have the Gospel preached unto them. Another reason why the people as a general thing were anxious to alter their churches; and this was one of the reasons that prompted this church to remodel their house. The old houses were not well ventilated, nor lighted. In order to secure all these advantages, so necessary to health as to comfort, it was determined at least to make some necessary alteration to the church. Every colored church in the city presented a very inviting appearance, becoming their means, however, this old church was an exception; it was the same old-fashioned house that it was forty-six years back, only as a matter of course a little the worse for wear; to change the appearance of things a little, and make this temple of worship more desirable and pleasant, prompted the people at least to make the attempt to remodel the interior, at this seeming unfavorable time, of which I am now writing as above referred to; the people, with a determination creditable to them, entered with a proper spirit into ways and means to accomplish their desire, under the lead particularly of Mr. Jacob C. White, Sen.; plans were proposed and adopted, and the operation commenced, and which they very soon accomplished at a cost of $1452 43 cts.

In this they were assisted by our church extension committee to the amount of four hundred dollars. In the short space of three months the work was accomplished, and will in point of neatness compare very favorably with any of our sister churches; not the least interesting part of the effort is the fact that when the work was completed it was paid for, so that the church was relieved from debt, and remains so until the present time. I must, however, say that there was not only a unity of action by the majority of the people to remodel the interior of the house, but a willingness to contribute of their money for the purpose, yet withal, to Mr. White particularly belongs the direction and control of the successful effort. Considering then the motive that influenced the congregation to remodel the house, they cannot be charged with an undue pride. The other churches were commodious and attractive, and showed improvement; they wore an aspect so pleasing that it proved an inducement to the young to resort to them. This house alone stood as it does now on the exterior, like an antiquated relic of gone by days, remembered as a place where amid the musty memories of the past it is remembered however venerated it may be regarded, yet it was not in keeping with the progress of the times when progress is the watchword, in fact "the lamp now that burneth" and shines so distinctly athwart our pathway. True, the old church always retained a hold upon the respect of the community; its character for order and consistency unquestioned, and among the churches none are regarded as retaining more of the simplicity of Christian requirements in their externals than this old church, for there are many in it whose regular attendance for worship to this house is proverbial, and as it is in attendance, so in everything else; in dress, in general conduct, in temperance, in worship, in conversation, avoiding all show of parade, avoiding all of those trappings and harness lately introduced into the Church of Christ in the forms of bills of fare, such as fairs, mental feasts, suppers, or teas as they are called, and those destructive ones under the significant head of "great attraction;" then follow theatrical displays, as Sabbath School exhibitions—the majority of pieces spoken taken from dramatic writers, not from God's Word, neither Christian writers nor poets; these are too tame for those training in these schools of Christ. The very dress in which many appear is the drapery of the stage, the glitter and show of the theatre—by no means the .simple, neat, becoming one of the Christian, which, in order to be consistent and sincere in profession, should be observed. Against all these outrages this old church is set, from them they have "washed their hands in innocency," against them all it "lifts up its voice;" within its holy precincts they cannot enter. I have given a reason why the interior of the church was remodelled, and the like reason may be presumed why before very long some alteration should be made to the outside appearance of the building, for it presents anything else than an inviting one. We are in hope that not many months more and the appearance of the entire superstructure will be changed, but not by any of the trappings above alluded to; only from Christian principles will it be attempted. The remodelling of the inside being completed the place was dedicated to the service of God on the seventh of May, 1854. Rev. R. Happerset preached the opening sermon in the morning. Dr. Joseph H. Jones preached in the afternoon. Both were listened to by large congregations.

The next course for the further interest of the Church, and, we hope, for the glorious extension of our Redeemer's kingdom, was to call a minister to take the pastoral oversight of the church; consequently, at a meeting of the session, held March the 20th, 1855, Dr. Joseph H. Jones, Moderator, it was agreed that a congregational meeting should be held on Friday evening, the 23d inst., for the call of a pastor. Said meeting was held, when the Rev. Wm. T. Catto was nominated and elected; the call was made out and presented to Presbytery, of which the pastor elect was a member; the call being accepted, Presbytery appointed the 22d April as the time of installation, Dr. Lewis Cheeseman to preach the sermon, Dr. Joseph H. Jones to deliver the charge to the people, Dr. Henry Steele Clark the charge to the pastor, all of which was done. The sermon on the occasion was from Heb. v. 1, 2 verses, and will never be forgotten by the writer of this history, neither by the dense mass of human beings who thronged the church to its utmost capacity upon that memorable occasion. If the hearty responses and warm greetings of the multitude, if the cordial shake of the hand as the right hand of fellowship was given, if the cheerful smiles of some and the deep emotions of others are any proofs of cordial welcome, and should act as reasons why the relation of pastor and people should be perpetuated, then the strongest reasons exist that the pastor and his flock will dwell together as brethren in Christ, and in the unity of the spirit and bond of faith, which may God grant.

It is not for me now to say what are the future prospects of the church; this must be left for the future historian to record when I too shall be called hence to sleep the sleep of death. It remains for me to record that the church at present comprises a membership of one hundred and eighty-two persons who are communicant members; these, together with others who are pew-holders and stated worshippers, present, at present, a very interesting congregation; there are three ruling elders, Mr. Thomas Black, John Birch, and Jacob C. White. Thirteen trustees govern the finances of the church, and they so manage the affairs of the church through the tact of their foreman, Mr. James Clay, that it can be said they "owe no man anything." Connected with the church is a Sabbath-school, numbering about forty scholars, Mr. J. C. White being the superintendent, assisted by Mrs. Sarah Hawkins. From this school, established by Mr. Gloucester, have risen up and gone forth, bearing precious seed, several ministers of the Gospel; Mr. Gloucester's four sons, all of whom were ministers, were children of this school. Jeremiah, Stephen, and John have each finished their work, and ere this I hope are with their beloved and honored father resting in peace; James, the youngest, is still alive and living in New York, a member of one of the New School Presbyteries in that city. Mr. Henry Wilson and Jonathan Gibbs, both pastors of churches, one in New York City, the other in Troy, State of N. Y., were both children of this school; and there are some now preaching in other denominations who were raised up and trained here. There is now at the Ashmun Institute, established by the New Castle Presbytery, and located in Oxford, West Chester County, Mr. Thomas Amos, a young man taken up by this church, and recommended to our Presbytery, who was received after examination, and is now prosecuting his studies with a view to the Gospel ministry. Surely, then, the old church is not without its interest and its history. What may be its future is with Him alone who sees from the beginning and knows the ending; it is but for the church to labor on in the good work of the Lord, that we review often the past and learn lessons of instruction to guide into the future; and amid all to look to Him who is head of His Church, and to Jesus, the author of faith, our Prophet, Priest, and King, to whom be glory in the Church forever.

Amen.

NOTE.—It may not be amiss for me to record, in connection with this history, some instances of pure benevolence shown this church. First, at the time when a claim for debt, said to be due to Mr. John Gloucester, the founder, was laid against the church, and the sheriff was about to execute a sale of the property to pay said claim, Mr. Chauncy, a gentleman of large benevolence, gave as a donation $700 to settle the debt, and this saved the property.

In 1839, Mr. J. Williams, a member of the Sixth Presbyterian Church, Dr. J. H. Jones, pastor, by will left $500 to the church.

The Demosthenes Society (colored) also gave a donation of $60 for the use of the trustees.

Subsequently, 1849, Dr. Ashbel Green left by will $50 for the church, and an equal sum for Rev. C. W. Gardner, formerly the pastor.

APPENDIX.

Conceiving that a synoptical history of all the colored churches in the city of Philadelphia, would be of some interest to the reader, I have undertaken to insert in this work when each church was founded, the number of members at present, the size of each building, also the value of each, and a short account of any matter that may be of interest.

There are in the city 18 churches, to wit:—

1. A. M. E. BETHEL CHURCH.

This church is located in South Sixth Street, east side, between Lombard and Pine. It was founded in 1816 as an African M. E. Church by Richard Allen; it is a large brick edifice substantially built, plain, but neat; it is 62 feet wide, 70 feet long, with a basement story divided into a lecture room, class rooms, and minister's study with a library attached. The church and lot upon which it stands, together with other property owned by the corporation, are at the lowest possible estimate, valued at $60,000; the audience room is very capacious, and for neatness is equalled but by few churches in the city; it is rated to seat about 2500 persons. The church is composed of 1100 communicant members. It has a Sabbath school containing 350 children, 2 superintendents, and 25 teachers (11 males and 14 females). This church was the first African Methodist Episcopal Church organized in the United States; its branches at present extend nearly over the whole Union. The aggregate membership is about 30,000. Rt. Rev. Richard Allen was the first bishop; since, there have been five more ordained, to wit, Rt. Revds.

Edward Waters, Morris Brown, Wm. Paul Quinn, Willis Nazry, and Daniel A. Payné; the three last are at present the acting bishops, the others being dead.

2. UNION A. M. E. CHURCH.

This church is located in Coates St., N. L., between Fifth and Fourth Streets. It is a brick edifice, 68 feet long, by 38 feet wide; it has a basement in which are a lecture room and two class rooms. The audience room is very tastefully finished, well ventilated, and will compare with any of our churches for neatness. It was founded in 1816, and at present contains a membership of 297 communicants; the church is rated to seat 800 persons. It has a Sabbath-school attached, with 160 scholars, 10 male teachers, and 8 females. There is a fine library attached to the school. The building and lot are valued at $14,000.

3. A. M. E. WESLEY CHURCH.

This is a neat little brick superstructure located in Hurst St. between Lombard and South, Fifth and Sixth Streets; it will seat about 500 persons. The church was founded in 1834; there are 300 members. There is also a basement to this building, in which are a lecture room, three class rooms, and a minister's studio. There is a Sabbath-school of 27 children, 3 male and 2 female teachers. The entire property is valued at $6,000.

4. AFRICAN M. E. MISSION.

This is a brick building 22 feet long by 18 feet wide. The building and lot are valued at $800, will seat 250 persons. This mission was commenced in 1852; at present there is a membership of 120 persons. In the Sabbath-school are 68 children. The mission is under the charge of the Rev. Stephen Smith, the city missionary of the A. M. E. Church. The church is located in South Seventh Street, below Dickson St., Southwark.

5. A. M. E. ALLEN CHAPEL.

A wooden building 20 feet long by 16 wide, and together with the lot is valued at $400. It is situated in Christian Street below

South Second Street; it contains a membership of 30 persons, and will accommodate 150 persons with seats. Attached is a Sabbath-school of 28 children. This mission is also under the care of Rev. S. Smith.

6. ZOAR METHODIST EPISCOPAL CHURCH.

This church is situated in Brown St., N. L., between Fifth and Fourth Streets, and is in connection with the M. E. Church. Supposed to have 150 members, and Sabbath-school children, 75. The building is of brick; will seat about 400 persons; has a basement with lecture room and two class rooms. The edifice is about 60 feet long, by about 35 wide. The audience room is plain and well finished. It has no side galleries, but one on the end. Valued about $12,000.

7. ST. THOMAS PROTESTANT EPISCOPAL.

This edifice is of brick, and stands at the corner of Adelphi and Fifth St., between Locust and Walnut. The building is about 60 feet long, and about 40 wide. There is a large lecture room and minister's library in the basement. The audience room is a fine specimen of architectural finish, differing materially from the finish of the other churches. Attached to the building is a vestry room. There are 337 adult members in communion. The building in the audience room will seat on the lower floor and galleries, about 800 persons. The church has attached an interesting Sabbath-school of 145 children, 5 males, and seven females, teachers. It was founded in 1794. Wm. Gray, Absalom Jones, Wm. White, Wm. Gardner, Henry Stewart, and Wm. Wiltshire, were the founders and trustees. The entire property, including the large lot upon which the church stands, together with the parsonage, is valued at $40,000.

8. WESLEY METHODIST CHURCH.

This is a neat brick edifice, located in Lombard St., between South Sixth and Fifth Sts.; it was founded in 1820, Mr. Josiah Blue at the time the minister. The building is 60 feet long, 42 wide, and is rated to seat 800 persons. For style and finish it is not surpassed by any of the colored churches in Philadelphia. There are 500 communicant members. Attached is a Sabbath-school of 165 children, 10 males and 12 females, teachers. This building, also, has a basement with class rooms and minister's study. The entire property is valued at $20,000.

9. ISRAEL CONGREGATIONAL METHODIST.

This building stands at the corner of South Fifth and Gaskill Sts., between Lombard and South Sts. It is a very old brick edifice, and wears a very antiquated appearance inside and out. It is a large edifice, being 72 long, and 41 feet wide. It has no basement; will seat about 2,000 persons. It was founded as a Congregational church in 1850. There are about 200 members to this church. Property valued about $18,000.

10. JOHN WESLEY M. E. CHURCH.

This church is in Shippen St. between Seventh and Eighth Sts. It is a small brick building 45 feet long by 23 feet wide. The church was founded in 1844, by Rev. Geo. Valentine. There are at present 100 members. It will seat about 200 persons. This property is valued at $4,000.

11. 1st AFRICAN BAPTIST CHURCH, FOUNDED IN 1830.

This is the first colored Baptist Church organized in Philadelphia, Rev. Mr. King being the founder. The house is of brick; in the interior or audience room it may be said to be beautiful to behold. The building is 48 feet by 40. It will seat about 350 persons. The property is valued at $5,000. It is located in Pearl St. near Eleventh and between Vine and Wood Sts. There are 200 members belonging to this church, mostly young persons; there are 130 children in the Sabbath-school.

12. UNION BAPTIST CHURCH.

Was founded in 1832 by the Rev. Daniel Scott. There are at present 260 members, with a Sabbath-school attached of 97 scholars, 9 teachers, 4 males and five females. The edifice is of brick, 51 by 32 feet; it has a basement with lecture room and minister's studio. The audience room will accommodate about 500 persons. In appearance, either inside or out, this church will compare favorably with any of our churches. It is located in Little Pine St., between South Sixth and Seventh Sts. The property is valued at $5,000.

13. SHILOH BAPTIST CHURCH.

Located near corner Clifton and South Sts. Was organized in 1842, Rev. John F. Raymond, minister. The building is of brick, 54 by 40 feet in dimension ; it has a basement with lecture room and minister's studio. The audience room is of plain, neat finish, and will seat comfortably about 600 persons. There are 225 members in communion with this church. A Sabbath-school with 85 scholars and 8 teachers, 7 of which are females. The entire property is valued at $11,000.

14. CHURCH OF THE CRUCIFIXION.

This church was organized in 1850, and is under the Protestant Episcopal Mission, better known as the Episcopal Mission Station, and under the supervision of the Rev. George Bringhurst. It is located in South Eighth St., between Shippen and South. It is a brick building about 55 feet long by 40 feet wide, and will seat about 500 persons. There is no basement; the audience room being on the first floor, includes the entire inner space from the floor to the rafters, which gives it a very airy as well as commodious appearance. The finish is very plain, though neat; it has recently been remodelled. This church was originally intended for poor colored people, and was to be considered a free church as it still is ; but such was the increase of white people upon the ministry of Mr. Bringhurst, that it was found necessary to receive white persons to membership. There are, however, in communion with this church 50 colored members, 300 colored Sabbath-school children, taught by 20 white teachers, males and females, who have devoted their attention and time to their religious culture. In connection, there is a day (parochial) school, comprising 80 scholars.

15. UNION METHODIST CHURCH.

Located in Little Pine St. between Sixth and Seventh Sts. Was founded in 1837 ; contains about 100 members. The house is a small brick building, about 18 feet wide, and about 40 feet long, and valued at $2,000. It was founded by Rev. Peter Spencer.

16. 1st AFRICAN PRESBYTERIAN CHURCH.

This building stands on South Seventh St., near the corner of Shippen St. The exterior of this building is very plain, the interior very creditable; as it has been very recently remodelled. It will seat very comfortably about 900 persons. The church was founded in 1807, and at present numbers about 180 communicant members. There is a Sabbath-school attached, consisting of 61 children, 2 male and 3 female teachers. There is a library attached of 271 volumes. The property is valued at $8,000.

17. SECOND PRESBYTERIAN CHURCH.

This is a fine, modern built brick edifice, 37 by 51, located in St. Mary St., between South Sixth and Seventh Sts., founded in 1824, then Old School, but now under the New School. The interior of the church is very neat; it will seat about 450 persons comfortably. There is a basement to this church; it is divided into lecture room, session room, and a minister's studio. Through a division that took place whereby nearly one-half of the members left, there are now but 75 persons members of the church. There is a Sabbath-school connected with the church, containing 30 children, 3 male and 3 female teachers. The property is valued at $6,000.

18. CENTRAL PRESBYTERIAN CHURCH.

This church was founded in 1844 by Rev. Stephen Gloucester, a son of Rev. John Gloucester. The edifice is a very fine brick building, tastily finished externally. Within, it is very handsomely completed in its architecture and furniture. The building is 60 feet long by 38 feet wide, and will seat comfortably about 600 persons. It has a basement with a lecture room, session room, and minister's studio, with a fine library attached. There are 260 members in communion. There is a Sabbath-school of 75 children, 6 male and 6 female teachers. The property is valued at $15,000.

To sum up the aggregate of all these churches, we arrive at the following result:—

18 churches capable of accommodating 11,000 persons.

4354 communicant members.

1615 children taught in the sabbath-schools.
Value of church property, $227,200.

When we consider that there are in the city of Philadelphia about 30,000 people of color, we see there is still room for further effort in filling up these churches. And may we not hope that God's blessing will still be upon us, and, trusting upon his favor and loving kindness, and with hearts filled with thankfulness for his past mercies, go forward, and, with united hearts, do with all our might what our hands find to do. And now unto Him that is able to do exceeding abundantly above all that we ask or think, according to the power that worketh in us, unto Him be glory in the Church by Jesus Christ throughout all ages world without end. Amen.

www.ingramcontent.com/pod-product-compliance
Lightning Source LLC
LaVergne TN
LVHW021424110826
845150LV00007B/2080

* 9 7 8 1 4 2 5 5 0 8 4 6 3 *